WHAT SENIOR BANKERS SAY ABOUT ST. MEYER & HUBBARD

- "Your personal coaching and mentoring have done wonders for me as well as my team."
- "I have seen clear evidence of great progress and developing leadership within the associates that have been privileged to work with you. We will continue to utilize the tools you have equipped us with."
- "I thought, 'You can't teach an old dog new tricks.' I was wrong. I tried a new method to my sales pitch and found it comfortable."
- "I will be closing a comprehensive relationship at the end of this month as a result of your disciplined prospecting approach. It has become an integral part of my daily sales routine."
- "There's a 'straight-talk express' in banking and Jack Hubbard and Bob St. Meyer are driving it."
- "Coaching our coaches...that's where the long term value of our partnership will pay huge dividends."
- "Our bank has worked with some of the top consultants in the world. We've never seen the kind of practical help provided by St. Meyer & Hubbard. Sales are up 100 percent every year in some of our most important categories. We trust them as if they were part of our bank, and they are."

VOLUME ONE

Conversations with PROSPECTS

St. Meyer & Hubbard
PERFORMANCE CULTURE SERIES

VOLUME ONE

Conversations with PROSPECTS

The First Step Toward Sales Success

By Bob St. Meyer & Jack Hubbard

WINANS KUENSTLER PUBLISHING
Doylestown, Pennsylvania

ISBN: 978-0-9815411-0-5

To order copies:
St. Meyer & Hubbard
10N865 Williamsburg Drive
Elgin, Illinois 60124
(847) 717-4328
www.StMeyerandHubbard.com

Published by:
Winans Kuenstler Publishing, LLC
47 West Oakland Ave.
Doylestown, PA 18901
www.WKPublishing.com

First Edition
Printed in the United States of America

Contents

"You can make more friends in two months by becoming interested in other people than you can in two years by trying to get people interested in you."

—Dale Carnegie

Dedicated to the men and women in the financial services industry who put themselves on the line for their clients every day.

Acknowledgements

WRITING A BOOK while running a business is similar to rebuilding your home while living in it. There were many challenges that never showed up on the blueprint, but the result has been very satisfying.

We owe so much to so many, not only for help with this book but for our very existence as a company. Our families have lived with husbands and fathers who have been on the road forty-plus weeks a year for more years than they care to recall. They pack us, hug us and send us on our way with wishes for safe travel, and welcome us home with warmth and open arms. How can one ever repay that kind of selflessness?

We value our many advocates, and friends. Bankers like Brian O'Connor and Jonathan Rohde, who believed in us enough in early 2001 to become our first clients when our business model was still in the oven. They remain our partners to this day.

We are grateful to Tom Doherty, Judy Buchanan, Bill Hippensteel, and Steve Heine. They have all shared their valuable time as references on a regular basis. Friends like Nick Miller, President of Clarity Advantage; Bobby

Martin, President of First Research; Kent Stickler, President of Stickler Learning; Jim Donnelly, Professor Emeritus at University of Kentucky; Charles Wendel, Principle of FIC Consulting; and John Barlow and Linda O'Connell of Barlow Research—they have all contributed to our personal growth and will leave a lasting mark on the banking industry.

We acknowledge the great work of our competitors: Dr. Martin Cohen, CEO of Cohen-Brown Management Associates; the outstanding professionals at Omega Performance; Linda Richardson, CEO of Richardson and Company; and Marshall Weems, CEO of Financial Selling Systems. These and countless others have partnered with thousands of bankers over the last several decades to help optimize sales and sales management conversations in business banking, retail banking and wealth management.

It is an honor to have Charles Green, CEO of The Trusted Advisor, quoted here. Charlie helped coin the concept of the "trusted advisor," a role we strive to play in the business lives of all our clients. His book, "Trust Based Selling," should be required reading for every sales professional.

We are indebted to our world class St. Meyer & Hubbard team: a group of dedicated professionals who are at their desks before the sun rises, or in the field coaching and teaching bankers to hold better sales conversations:

Dwight Lampley, a gifted facilitator who heads our training and coaching practice;

Julie Ruffolo, Executive Vice President and the nation's finest retail banking sales coach;

Margi Miller, who leads our Performance Management division and never lets anything fall through the cracks;

Linda Benjamin, Senior Vice President, Performance Manager and one of the most energetic people we've known;

Kathy Kruzich, Senior Vice President, Performance Manager, who is constantly questioning the status quo and making us better;

Holly Sansone, the best developer in the industry;

Mike Dillon, Performance Coach, who has helped business bankers and investment professionals achieve extraordinary sales increases;

Joanne Krettick, our newest associate, whose quality work and methodical style are complemented by her steady demeanor.

Lisa Pawlowicz, Director of Client Experience, unfailingly loyal for over 15 years, continues to redefine client service and dedication;

Adam Hubbard, Graphics Coordinator, great with graphics, and even better as a son.

We appreciate the contributions of Foster Winans, our editor and collaborator, in bringing this book (and those to follow) to life.

Finally, we thank those who said "no" to us during our careers and those who thought or hoped we would fail or fall short of our goals. Your rejection of our concept of creating Performance Cultures through behavioral coaching challenged us, brought our team closer together and made us all stronger as individuals and as a company.

—Bob St. Meyer
Jack Hubbard
Elgin, Illinois 2008

About the Authors

BOB ST. MEYER, President of St. Meyer & Hubbard, is a banking and consulting veteran with more than three decades experience. He is regarded as one of the nation's leading sales facilitators and has taught more than 50,000 bankers.

St. Meyer earned his MBA from Xavier University in Ohio. His banking career included stints with National City Corporation, Florida National Bank, and First Union Corporation.

He has taught and coached bankers in retail, commercial, and wealth management divisions of Wachovia Corporation, Bank of America, Harris Bank, Fifth Third Bank, and more than four dozen community and regional financial services organizations.

A published author, he is a sought-after speaker, having appeared before the Bank Administration Institute and American Bankers Association, among others.

JACK HUBBARD, Chief Experience Officer of St. Meyer & Hubbard, has shared his passion for trust-based sales in the financial services industry for more than three decades. He has helped build performance cultures at more than 100 banks, including Wachovia Corporation, Bank of America, and Harris Bank.

With nearly 60,000 bankers personally trained and coached, Hubbard is a sought-after facilitator. In 2008 he returns for his 22nd consecutive year on the faculty of American Banking Association's School of Bank Marketing and Management.

Hubbard is also an instructor at the prestigious Stonier Graduate School of Banking, ABA's National Commercial Lending School, ABA's Graduate Commercial Lending School, Southwest Graduate School of Banking, and the North Carolina School of Banking. He is a regular presenter for national conferences and workshops sponsored by leading national and state industry associations. He has been a regular presenter at Crain's New York annual Small Business Conference.

Hubbard's articles regularly appear in such industry publications as "*Selling Power,*" "*The American Banker,*" "*Financial Services Marketing,*" "*ABA Bank Marketing Journal,*" "*Commercial Lending Review,*" and numerous state banking association journals. His monthly sales and sales management column appears in the "*RMA Journal.*"

Foreword

I WAS A COMMERCIAL BANKER in North Carolina in the 1990s when I had a conversation with a prospect that changed my life and career. The prospect was the CFO of an engineering firm and she was hastily explaining to me how her business and industry functioned, how much of their revenue went to payroll and other details. Her phone was constantly ringing, aides were coming and going, and her desk was piled with paperwork.

There I was, using up her limited time asking questions I should have done some research on first. I made a passing remark that, "It would be great if I knew all this before I came to see you." She agreed, and that launched me on a mission that resulted in my leaving banking to start a company, First Research, devoted to generating up-to-date intelligence about different industries that bankers could consult before calling on prospects.

Back in those days banks had started calling us "relationship managers." But it was a change in name only. We were still expected to meet that week's or that month's quota. My experience had taught me that selling would be a lot less stressful if I first established a true relationship with customers. If I knew what kept business executives awake at night, I would be more valuable to them than just another guy in a suit pushing the commodity product-du-jour.

Today, First Research has grown into a huge database fed by an army of analysts digging up the latest and most relevant news and information on more than seven hundred industry segments for clients in banking and other industries. But as valuable as our clients find our service, it's only as valuable as they make it. That is where Jack Hubbard and Bob St. Meyer come in.

As a former banker now in the business of helping bankers, I know that long-term business success is built on more than product and price. I had that instinct back in North Carolina when I turned my prospecting calls into information gathering.

What separates success from failure is an organizational state of mind built around a simple concept: the more you give, the more you receive. No one understands that concept better than Jack and Bob. They are industry missionaries, teaching people how to stop thinking about products and start thinking like *banker-preneurs* whose goal is to help customers achieve their goals.

In these pages you will find the distillation of the successful prospecting approach they have developed and teach, and all that I believe, about what goes into long term sales success. In an economy that places so much emphasis on quarter-to-quarter results, St. Meyer & Hubbard is teaching bankers that you can have your cake and eat it, too. It's much more complicated than that, and it takes a real commitment on the part of management, as well as the stomach to weather the criticism and pushback that often accompanies change. But it works.

We know that St. Meyer and Hubbard's *Trusted Advisor Prospecting System* (TAPS) works because we can correlate the success of our clients with whether or not they use it. Industry Intelligence is a tool within TAPS that drives success. Jack and Bob teach and coach bankers to use that tool in a thoughtful, integrated system that teaches relationship managers to become valued partners of their customers.

Instead of asking customers for business, they encourage bankers to study customers, listen to customers, and give customers a reason to do business. One way to do that is to be the eyes and ears for prospects, offering value up front without asking for anything in return; building trust. Prospects who learn to trust are motivated to buy. Prospects who learn to trust give you referrals. Prospects who learn to trust are almost disinterested in price, and very focused on the value you bring to their business lives.

I encourage you to read this primer on prospecting and begin to incorporate the lessons contained in it to grow yourself as a performance consultant. If you do, the results will surely follow.

—Bobby Martin, *President and Co-Founder*
First Research, Inc.
Raleigh, North Carolina 2008

Introduction

"One of the best ways to persuade others is with your ears."

—Dean Rusk (1909–1994), former U.S. Secretary of State

THE YEAR 2007 is likely to be remembered as one of the best and worst times for the banking industry.

On one hand, the crash of the subprime mortgage sector swept away competitors in real estate and commercial lending—hedge funds, private equity, mortgage brokers, investment banks. There has been a flight to safety—traditional banks are "in" again. Major investment firms have allocated or raised special pools of money to invest exclusively in community and regional banks.

On the other hand, a wave of mega-mergers has created competitors with deep pockets and long reaches who have been waging a ground war of branch building. The FDIC counted almost 95,000 branches in the U.S. in 2006, an increase of nearly 15 percent over a ten-year period. Meanwhile, new banks are springing up at a rapid rate. In 2006, 191 new FDIC banks opened their doors, the most since the year 2000.

Discount brokers are offering checking accounts and banks are offering brokerage accounts. Customers have gotten wise to the opportunities provided by the Internet to effortlessly move deposits—a bank's most profitable product—to take advantage of better returns elsewhere.

A lot has changed in banking, but one thing has stayed the same, through good times and bad: a sale begins with a conversation that may lead to a partnership, and a well-managed relationship still trumps rate wars, branch proliferation, media blitzes, direct mail campaigns, the Internet, and convenience. When it comes to money, most customers still prefer the human touch.

"*Conversations with Prospects*" is the first in a series of books that distill what we have learned about the elements of sales success during our decades of helping hundreds of banks and 250,000 bankers reinvent their sales culture, changing it from score-keeping and tick-marking to performance-driven. We know what works because our clients who have embraced the message and stuck with the process have reaped significant rewards in increased sales and profits. And what is the message?

The art of selling is not persuasion, it's conversation;
It's not about pitching, it's about catching;
It's not about closing the deal, it's about opening a relationship;
It's not about the volume of phone calls or visits a relationship manager makes, it's about the care, planning, and value that goes into the calls made.

None of these concepts by itself is ground-breaking. The power comes from integrating the tools, training, and coaching into a strategy, and then building a culture that focuses on and rewards performance. This is harder to do than it sounds, as evidenced by the growth in the number of conferences, schools, and training devoted to the subject. Culture is by definition a set of imbedded habits and attitudes and, as the wisdom goes, it is easier to create culture than to change it.

The lessons we've learned from our conversations and interactions with client bankers is that successful sales teams are those led by managers who understand that sustainable success requires more than a few training videos and some nifty technology. It is an ongoing, never-ending, constantly evolving process. It is a way of business life and a way of thinking that, for many institutions, remains a challenge.

"Too many banks waste too much time with inarticulate value positions, inconsistent sales processes, and ineffective sales management," says Nick Miller, founder of Clarity Advantage and a management consultant for the past three decades working with banking and other industries. He points to a Greenwich Associates survey that found just one in five small business owners could recall any details about a single bank sales call they had received.

"Ask most banks to state their value proposition and they talk about products. That's not true value. What they should be doing is talking about advising business people how to generate more money than they have, to accelerate their cash flow."

Thomas J. Doherty, Senior VP of Business Banking for Park National Bank, has observed that the banking industry is slowly moving from transactional selling to relationship-based selling. "But we still have a long way to go. Competition is keen and it's becoming hard to differentiate on a product basis. One bank's loans and deposits look a lot like another's. Everyone says the solution is to be better at service. But when you ask for specifics, they define it as 'I carry my cell phone on my belt and you can reach me any time.' "

We think of Tom Doherty and the other bank leaders we've worked with as pioneers in a landscape crawling with hostile forces. Senior bank managers are hobbled by old habits and attitudes. Bank culture changes at a glacial pace while customers are becoming more sophisticated every day. Margins are narrower and demands for profitability more insistent.

The future of banking belongs to the Tom Dohertys of the world, and to those who take to heart the common sense wisdom that is at the core of what we teach and coach. We invite you to join us on this journey and become part of that future.

—Bob St. Meyer & Jack Hubbard

PART I
From the Outside Looking In

Chapter 1: The Stakes

"The most important thing in communication is to hear what isn't being said."

Peter Drucker, author, business consultant (1909–2005)

TOM FELTENSTEIN is a marketing expert (a former protégé of the late Ray Kroc, founder of McDonald's) who preaches to his corporate audiences a concept he calls "neighborhood marketing."

All marketing is local, he argues, and most businesses don't get it. One of his pet peeves is banks.

> "Banks are about the worst at neighborhood marketing and it makes no sense since they do most of their business in their neighborhoods. They spend millions on advertising and I have yet to see a bank ad that didn't use the same tired wording or concept: 'Your Friendly Neighborhood Bank.'
>
> "The two banks I do business with have never been friendly enough to ask me about my business needs. You'd think that a bank would come and

> visit with me and say, 'Look, you're a really great customer. Here are the five services you use. Here are twenty more that we would like to tell you about. We would like to develop a further relationship. We know you have money set aside in a money-market. Why don't you let us set up a trust account through our trust department for your kids?'
>
> "They've got all these products, they know just about everything about me—how much business I do, what I spend, what I save, where I live. They've got a built-in market to sell the other products. It amazes me that they don't mine the gold they already have inside their four walls. Most customers are worth so much more to a bank."

If most businesses chose their bank the way they select their other vendors, a lot of banks would be in bigger trouble than they are. SurePayroll, a Chicago-based company that provides online payroll services, conducted a survey in early 2007 that found fewer than one in ten business owners chose their bank on the basis of products and rates. "Small business banking has become a commodity. With only a few exceptions, every bank offers the same products and services. It's no surprise that small business owners are not spending much time evaluating a bank's services."

While banking has become a commodity, customer time has become precious. Business leaders spend less time with vendors than any other of their responsibilities. A survey by Gold Group LLC, an Internet social networking agency, found that executive decision-makers spend on average 35 percent of their time on planning, budgeting, and business lines; 35 percent on outside stakeholders (from clients to trade associations); and another 25 percent on inside stakeholders (staff and management).

That leaves just 5 percent for vendors. If you're selling the same thing at about the same price as everyone else, you need to define how the experience of buying from you will be better than with the other guys. And you'll need to do it soon because it's increasingly what customers are demanding.

If you're selling the same thing at about the same price as everyone else, you need to define how the experience of buying from you will be better than with the other guys.

Forrester Research, the Cambridge, Massachusetts market research firm, released a major study in June 2007, conducted for American Banker magazine, headlined "*Banks Prepare for Customer Experience Wars.*" Forrester interviewed nearly two dozen large companies about their banking experiences, and nearly two hundred banking executives. The conclusion, similar to SurePayroll's, was that customer needs, not product features, are what count, and that banks aiming for organic growth (as opposed to mergers and acquisitions) must push for more innovative approaches and treat customer experience as a competence, "not a function."

Banks that fail to grasp this do so at great risk. Traditional banking's share of the nation's economic pie has been shrinking for half a century. In 1967, bank reserves equaled one quarter of the US monetary base—the money supply. In 2007, that slice had shrunk to just five percent.

The banking surveys and the loss of the nation's wallet confirm what we're seeing and hearing—banking has reached a crossroads. Big changes are afoot and those leaders and managers with the vision and the will to change their approach to business development—from a sales culture to a performance culture—are finding a world of opportunity to capture a larger share of the wallets they have, and to steal share back from non-bank vendors and slow-footed competitors.

The opportunity is there because many banks are operating on out-of-date principles and employing faulty, poorly-planned tactics. We know this from our work, but also as bank customers.

Jack was settling down at home to watch one of his favorite television programs one evening not so long ago when he was interrupted by the phone. He found himself in an uninvited conversation with a banker peddling a special rate on home equity loans. He recalls:

> "Being in the business of helping teach bankers about prospecting, I let the woman breathlessly read off her product sheet about the bank's great rates, the tax benefit, and how I could use the equity in my home to take a fun trip. She knew nothing about me, including that I travel forty-seven weeks a year. I'm not in the market for another reason to get on an airplane.
>
> "When she'd spouted all the points provided her on the script, I turned the tables and began to interview her. I asked how often she calls people in the evening, what the bank names these events, what training she received prior to the calls, what tools she had to improve her chances of success, and what coaching she was getting. She had never been asked those questions by a prospect and instead of hanging up and moving on to the next faceless name and phone number on her list, she rose to the occasion. She could tell I felt her pain.
>
> "With a heavy sigh and a dispirited note in her voice she explained that 'Call Nights' at the bank

> were regular events, when she and her colleagues were required to stay late and dial for dollars. 'We call 'em Sink or Swim Nights. No training, no tools, no coaching. Just pizza and soda. If we exceed our quota of loan applications, we get a $200 bonus.'
>
> "I wished her good luck, because that was about the best she could hope for given the clumsy way her bank was trying to generate business."

Bankers hate these hit-and-run call nights more than customers. The woman who called Jack was well-spoken, intelligent, and conscientious—just what you'd want in a customer-driven business. But her bank was squandering this precious resource on a badly-executed tactic guaranteed to drain her of enthusiasm and hope. Worse, it annoyed a lot of potential customers for whom the bank was now identified as an intruder into their private lives—just another telemarketer.

People outside banking often ask us how an industry can be so out of touch with contemporary prospecting and sales strategies and techniques. Those who have been in banking a long time know the answer. But for newcomers, it's helpful to briefly place where we are today in context.

People outside banking often ask us how an industry can be so out of touch with contemporary prospecting and sales strategies and techniques.

The issues facing bankers thirty years ago—increased competition, unfavorable spreads, difficulty recruiting top talent—are still with us today. Back then the economy was limping along, interest rates were spiking, and oil prices were out of control. Then came the thrift industry bubble and debacle, followed by major consolidations which made it harder for smaller banks to compete.

The response was to slash costs, in many cases by reducing the head count and redistributing the extra work among the remaining relationship managers. Some banks added insurance and investment products, trying to become one-stop shops—the wallet-share strategy. Where the strategy was poorly planned, the result was overworked employees who were expected to learn and sell all the new products, on top of the products they already had.

Ever since Wall Street became aggressive recruiters in the 1980s and 90s, banks have found it harder to compete for new talent. They couldn't match the dollars or the opportunity for growth. In some cases they have hired people with little or no financial background and taught them the business. This is a labor intensive and costly process, with no guarantee you aren't simply training your competitor's next relationship managers.

Others have tried the "buy versus build" approach—hire the top talent away from the other guys. But an extensive survey in 2006 by the Business Banking Board, a leading industry-funded think tank, found that relationship managers hired from other banks are about the same or slightly less productive than relationship managers who've stayed at one bank and have the same years of experience. "It is not time down the street, it's time in the seat that drives productivity," the report concluded.

The survey of 7,800 bankers at 49 institutions in the small business and middle market segments also found that there was only a weak relationship between time devoted to selling and new production of loans and deposits. This finding debunked another widely-held belief that if business bankers have more time to sell—and spend less time on administration—they'll produce more "footings" (the sum of deposits and loans they generated). But it turns out that's not the answer either.

The Business Banking Board report concluded: "[A] misalignment exists…because the questions of acquiring experienced talent and creating sales time are the wrong questions to ask—they will never solve your productivity problems."

"…the questions of acquiring experienced talent and creating sales time are the wrong questions to ask–they will never solve your productivity problems."

The answer, according to some of the senior managers interviewed, is to hire more relationship managers. "I can't grow the business without taking on more staff," one was quoted as having complained. "I might get away with it for a year, but after that, my relationship managers would leave if I under-resourced the business any longer." Staffing up is a hard sell in the best of times, and heresy when margins are tight and stockholders are demanding consistent profitability and growth.

Sell Is Not A Four-Letter Word

One of banking's early sales pioneers is Kent Stickler, who has devoted his career to proving that our industry can be just as competitive and profitable as any other. He's been at it for more than four decades, serves on the faculty of eight banking schools, and speaks frequently on the subject. He offered us his unique perspective on the past, and a glimpse into the future.

"Banking has been slow to catch on to sales. I started in the business in 1968 and in the mid-1970s went to work for a community bank with the title of general sales manager. At conferences, people I'd hand my card to were often a little skeptical—sales was almost a swear word in banking.

"It used to be an easy business. If you earned a steady return on assets of 1.7% and showed growth of four to five percent a year, you felt no pain. Sales weren't necessary for survival. Now, banks are struggling to grow.

"The bank I was sales manager for in the 1970s got some attention in the trade press for our pioneering approach and I was invited to teach a Bank Marketing Association course. People came up to me after the class and asked, 'Could you help my bank?' So I ended up teaching bankers how to sell. Thirty years later, too many bankers still don't realize they are in the sales business.

"Instead, many community banks remain fixated on public relations and advertising. Ninety percent of their marketing dollars go into advertising. What good does it do to advertise a product if the bankers aren't prepared to sell it when the customer comes in the door?

"There are some visionary CEOs out there who have seen the future and are guiding their banks along the right path. But for every visionary, there are a lot of boards and executives who still haven't gotten the message. A principal problem is that the people who run banks today got their start thirty or so years ago and typically came up the ranks from operations or lending. They have never had to sell anything. They know how to run a bank, but not how to grow one.

"While the banking industry coasted along, the competition has been stealing business. It's common today for customers to have $10,000 in their checking account and several hundred thousand in a brokerage account. The older generations may still be hanging on to their jumbo CDs, but guess who's calling them about other opportunities? The brokerage industry. Meanwhile, try convincing a thirty-five-year-old to put money in a bank CD. They'll look at you like you're an idiot.

"The older generations may still be hanging on to their jumbo CDs, but guess who's calling them about other opportunities? The brokerage industry."

"Most traditional banks aren't speaking to customers who have money. The old model was to sit there and wait for someone to ask a question and run the credit check and open the account. Banks figured by building a lot of branches, they'd get the business they need through location alone. But the Wall Street brokers and other competitors weren't sitting around, and they've carved off a lot of business without much effort.

"The traditional bank offering of checking, savings, and loans is going to disappear. I'm often reminded of a seminal study in the mid-1970s by the late Theodore Levitt, a Harvard professor who coined the term 'globalization,' and authored the best-selling book 'Guerilla Marketing.'

"Levitt wrote about the four conditions that

guarantee the self-deceiving cycle of bountiful expansion and undetected decay. The banking industry has met all four. They are: the belief that an expanding and more affluent population assures growth; the belief that no competitive substitute exists for the industry's major product; too much faith in mass production and in the advantages of rapidly declining unit costs as output rises; and preoccupation with a product that lends itself to carefully controlled scientific experimentation and improvement.

"In every case Levitt cited, growth was threatened or stopped not because the market was saturated but because of management. For example, if you had told the American railroad industry fifty years ago they'd one day depend on federal subsidies to underwrite passenger service, they'd have thought you were insane. Levitt said the problems they encountered were not that people weren't traveling anymore. It was that they saw themselves as being in the railroad business when they should have defined themselves as being in the transportation business.

"If we define what we do as business banking, it won't be sustainable. But if we define our business as the financial industry, it's a whole different ball game. The need for investment and financial advice is greater than it's ever been, especially for baby boomers.

"I tell people not to get too down on banking. I'd start a bank today, but not a traditional bank. I'd go to Naples, Florida or wherever the market is growing, and I'd give it a non-bank name, stock it with sales people, and go up against some of these stodgy institutions that aren't getting it. The future's quite bright, if you understand where the opportunities are and are prepared to go after them."

The Fear Factor

According to Charles H. Green, author of "Trust-Based Selling," one of the biggest obstacles to changing culture is a negative bias people have toward the concept of selling.

> "The social dynamic is me versus them. The internal conversation is, 'How do I get someone else to do something that I want and not let them know what I'm doing?
>
> "This bias against talking about sales as sales is so strong that some organizations actually ban the use of the word sell. Instead many companies have adopted the euphemism 'business development'. But it's still sales.
>
> "Ask any group of five people to close their eyes and visualize selling and I guarantee a third will come up with the used car salesman. They can tell you what he's wearing and the pattern of the suit. These are deeply embedded stereotypes."

Another psychological hurdle Green identifies is the desire to appear smart and in control.

> "This leads us to talk way too much instead of being curious and listening. But doing that seems counter-intuitive. If you want to drive to an outcome, just listening seems like you're not controlling the outcome.

"We're taught to go into every meeting with an objective—know what you want. But that gets in the way of having an open dialogue. Most sales training feeds this by talking about sales process, CRM systems, and boxes that you check that say, Yes, we did this.

"These systems are said to make the sales process more efficient but that's a euphemism for screening or qualifying leads. This is anti-relationship. If your objective is to quickly find out whether a lead is going to be any good and immediately discard the ones who might waste your time, that's a hell of an attitude to approach people with.

"The perfect analogy is the young guy who is looking for a playmate. He screens all the dating service leads and as soon as he figures out he's not going to get lucky fast with a girl, he gets rid of them. Of course he never puts himself out like that. He talks about romance and candlelight and literature. But his real agenda is short-term results.

"But if a guy seriously wants to have a physical relationship, why not invest in romance and love? Then you'll end up with all the intimacy you want, but not if you go looking for it directly. It's socially inappropriate.

"We have created a socially inappropriate mode of relationship called selling which succeeds in turning off everybody. The salesman comes in and is looking at his watch and mumbling about quotas and talking about the prospect needing to sign something by Friday. This makes the buyer feel like he's being hustled."

Green says it takes some doing to get managers to grasp that, "selling costs get reduced in a relationship context, and you only generate relationships if you're willing to look past your nose and past the next transaction. You've got to have give and take. There has to be room for reciprocity and the only way to get reciprocity is looking beyond the immediate transaction."

"We have created a socially inappropriate mode of relationship called selling which succeeds in turning off everybody."

—Charles H. Green, Author of "Trust-Based Selling"

Chapter 2: Being a Banker Instead of a Bank

"Marketing is an attitude, not a department."

—Phil Wexler, author and lecturer

THE TITLE OF THIS BOOK includes the word "conversations" because it is the core concept of everything we teach.

Conversing with prospects—as opposed to pitching, making cold calls, holding a monthly sales blitz or dialing for dollars—is not a new idea. Business bookshelves are full of volumes devoted to aspects of this phenomenon, with titles such as "Selling Sucks," "Selling is Dead," "Cold Calling for Cowards," "Never Cold Call Again," and "The Little Red Book of Selling." Each of these contains advice ranging from tricks to get around telephone gatekeepers to full-scale relationship selling.

We think of the interaction between a banker and a prospect as a conversation in which both the banker and the prospect are doing more than listening to each other—they hear what's being said and find where their interests converge.

The conversations we teach bankers about never begin with a rate sheet, marketing collateral, or any mention of what the bank has to offer or sell. Instead, the conversation begins before the conversation takes place—with research, a plan, and an agile mind. And it has nothing to do with the bank. It's all about the prospect. (We describe some of the pre-conversation techniques we teach in Chapter 4.)

We teach bankers and bank managers to stop thinking of themselves as "the bank"—a soldier in an army of salespeople with a basket of products to sell and quotas to meet. We encourage them to start thinking like bankers in the true sense of the word: providers of services that are just as important—and just as personal—as medical care or legal advice.

People rarely shop for a doctor or a lawyer. The ones we end up using are most often referrals by family or business associates. However we find them, once we feel we've found a good doctor or a good lawyer, we tend to stick with them. Price becomes a secondary issue. We expect to pay more for trustworthiness, reliability, and accessibility.

People rarely shop for a bank, either, but when they do, it's not the bank's trustworthiness they care about. They chase rates and when they need a loan they're shopping for the path of least resistance. What bank shoppers usually find are sales people pushing products, when what many businesses really need is financial advice.

People rarely shop for a bank, but when they do, it's not the bank's trustworthiness they care about.

Like medical advice, financial advice is not just about the issue at hand, but about counseling and guidance. Barbara Kahn, a professor of marketing at Wharton School of Business, recently conducted research into how consumers make important health care decisions and found that patients had no trouble identifying the most important factors—quality of life, survival rates, and cost—but they struggled to express them in a single value.

The choices that must be made around financial advice are somewhat similar to health care issues in that they are often unpleasant or anxiety-producing, and difficult to express in a single value. If they could, bank customers would say they want someone who can help them make good choices. They want someone who will not just listen to them, but work in partnership to help the business grow, today and tomorrow. This is collaboration, the second "C" of selling, after the first "C," conversation.

If they could, bank customers would say they want someone who can help them make good choices. They want someone who will not just listen to them, but work in partnership to help the business grow, today and tomorrow.

If you ask most bankers today, "What's your value proposition?" many will default to a discussion about products or location or some variation on customer service. They may respond with something they memorized from a training class or reel off the script they were given by the marketing department. The correct answer is that bankers should be advising business people on how to generate more profits, accelerate their cash flow, and match their financing needs with their business strategies.

The bank of the future—which is being invented today at institutions like Bank of America, Umqua, Wachovia and community banks like Bangor Savings—is the bank envisioned by Kent Stickler: a financial services practice where each banker knows his customers well and handles their financial lives holistically, instead of product-by-product, in silos, by cycles, and so on. It's much more complicated than that, but those who have figured it out are beating the heck out of the competition.

Wall Street, wealth management advisors, mortgage companies, big banks, little banks, and even local investment pools have been marketing prospects to death by every means possible except with a conversation. But conversation is much more profitable, as a pioneering group of wealth managers has already proven.

CEG Research, a consulting firm catering to the financial advisor industry, recently completed a study for Dow Jones & Co. of more than 2,000 wealth managers, finding that those who invested their time in developing close client relationships control twice the assets and earn three times as much as traditional advisors. In "Best Practices of Elite Advisors: The Wealth Management Edge," CEG reported that the business model these high-performing wealth managers use allowed them to achieve faster growth by serving "many" fewer clients. Incredibly, "Only a small group of advisors truly practice the relationship-oriented, process-driven approach that defines wealth management."

This suggests a big opportunity for bankers. The CEG survey found that fully two-thirds of financial advisors are generalists who "try to be all things to all people," and do little consulting. Another 22 percent are niche product specialists who do no consulting. Only 7 percent of wealth managers rely on "a defined process and a high level of client communication. [Their clients] entrust them with a larger percentage of their assets and provide more referrals for new high-net-worth clients."

CEG found that the most successful wealth managers contacted top clients more than fifteen times a year, almost three times more often than investment generalists. When you learn how it works, conversation sells.

Ask Instead of Tell

What do prospects and customers want to hear? It varies widely. Some want advice. Some are price shoppers. There are business owners and finance executives who would never change banks because they value the people they deal with.

But one thing all prospects want is the same thing any of us want in our most valuable personal relationships. They want to be visible. They need a bank, but they want a banker—someone who knows who they are, what they do, and what are their challenges and opportunities.

Bankers often try too hard to prospect using techniques that are all about the bank, relying on persuasion instead of conversation. Unless the banker gets lucky and hits the prospect at a moment of desperation or unfulfilled need, the prospect invariably pushes back with any number of brush offs, but most often the shut-down line: "I'm happy with my present bank."

Bankers often try too hard to prospect using techniques that are all about the bank, relying on persuasion instead of conversation.

Bankers will introduce themselves to prospects by saying things such as, "I'd like to come out and introduce myself because I think I can save you some money." Or, "I'd like to discuss our cash management offerings." Who really needs to spend time listening to another banker peddling the same products as the rest of the pack? We see a lot of sales letters that are just as bad, talking about the sales person and company, but not the potential customer and their issues.

Customers have a well-defined list of basic financial needs, and each begins with the word "manage":

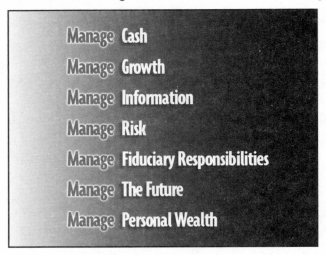

Manage Cash
Manage Growth
Manage Information
Manage Risk
Manage Fiduciary Responsibilities
Manage The Future
Manage Personal Wealth

Needs are not products. Bankers that discover, create, and exceed the need will always have business. Instead, many bankers dive into the process with a solution long before they have grasped the need. This may occur because of pressure from sales managers to hit their revenue numbers. When the push to sell products overrides the best interests of the client there is little discussion about managing anything.

When sales people are measured solely on the basis of production, the client is the ultimate loser.

In trust-based selling, the sales person stops trying to be interesting and learns to be interested. Banks that understand this work hard to focus on and understand the buying cycle of their prospects and clients. When banks match their sales cycle to the customer's buying cycle, it's a trust connection and they are well on their way to a sale.

The buying cycle is a five-step process the prospect or client goes through to arrive at a decision.

First, the business owner becomes aware that there is a need for a financial service. They may have outgrown their current bank's capacity to fulfill a particular need (such as how they manage their cash) or other circumstances may have changed that have rendered a bank's product inappropriate or obsolete.

The second step is to recognize that some action must be taken. For example, a business owner may realize that managing payroll is outside their area of expertise. The owner muddles along until he or she receives a nasty-gram from the IRS about an error in their tax payments. The owner realizes it's time to get some outside help.

The third buying cycle step is to evaluate the options. These days that often means searching the Internet first. Prospects today are generally better informed about what the options are before they ever talk to a banker. Research is but a click away, and that kind of knowledge doesn't require calling a bank and getting trapped in a sales pitch when what's really needed is help and advice.

The fourth stage is resolving concerns. The business owner must choose what's best for them. Customers hate making bad decisions, and their goal is to avoid buyer's remorse.

The final step is to implement the solution and make the purchase.

In some cases, the need is immediate or urgent. If the firm that's managing a customer's 401-K program has a reporting issue or a technology meltdown, such as a hacker corrupting the fiduciary's accounting system, the customer may decide it's time to move the 401-K elsewhere.

But if the customer is satisfied with his 401-K program, and a banker calls claiming his bank has a better 401-K, one with special bells and whistles, the customer is unlikely to want to rock the boat. That banker might have to call on that business owner for two years to get the sale. Most bankers will have given up long before that two years is up. They don't understand the wave-length of the buying cycle.

When the business owner's buying cycle is ahead of the banker's sales cycle, the banker might have to shorten the time between calls to catch up. More typically, the banker is far ahead of the prospect's buying cycle. It is not unusual for the prospect to perceive no need. Then it is the burden of the sales banker to alert the prospect to an unforseen need, such as managing risk. When this happens, the likelihood of prospects shopping other banks for a solution is much lower.

Bankers say they want a greater share of the customer's wallet. Our philosophy is to think of it as "share of relationship." The way to get there is through the heart—through ongoing conversations, holistic advice, getting to the personal side of the business, paying attention to customer habits, understanding buying cycle issues, and all the rest that we've discussed to this point. It all comes down to trust.

"You just need to do the right thing for clients. That has to be the priority."

Or as Jordan A. Miller, Senior Vice President of Fifth Third Bank, recently told *The American Banker* magazine for an article on tearing down silos, "You just need to do the right thing for clients. That has to be the priority."

Amen.

Chapter 3: Where the Buffalo Roam

"It is the service we are not obliged to give that people value most."

—James Cash Penney, founder, JC Penney

RELATIONSHIP MANAGERS (RMs) are the frontline in the quest for business banking wallet and market share. As such, they are engaged in several conversations at once. One is with their internal partners: managers, peers, support staff, and themselves.

We discuss some of these internal issues in more detail in Part Two, but generally banks that fail to meet the needs of the market and meet their goals are often those whose strategies are unclear, misaligned, or badly executed; whose cultures are defined by quotas and tick marks instead of goals and performance; whose infrastructures are inadequate to support the sales team; and those which are so preoccupied with internal issues that they can't hear what the market is asking: what's in it for me?

Good salesmanship is a bit like being a good hunter. If you've ever watched a cat stalking a squirrel or a bird,

you know that the cat spends a great deal of time watching its prey, tensed to spring, creeping ever closer until that precise moment when instinct tells it that the distance is short enough and it will be fast enough to justify the expenditure of energy to strike. Banking is not much different.

What to a predator is stalking, for a sales person is studying the market, targeting opportunities, listening to prospects, and learning what customers want. And the first place for most banks to begin that process is in their own back yards.

For example, one of our client banks conducts a regular exercise called Customer Check-ins. Several evenings a month, branch associates stay late and dial the phone, not for dollars, but for information. They call select customers of the bank to learn if there are other ways the bank can be of help, and how customers feel about their experiences with the bank—not what products they might buy.

There are no prizes for selling the most products, but there is a prize for the person who conducts the best conversation, as measured by the number of questions asked. The bankers are specifically instructed to refrain from talking about products unless it's unavoidable or logical. The goal of the calls is to ask trust-related questions—to have a conversation in which the customer is the star of the show, not the banker.

Before the Customer Call-In session, the team working that night holds a "huddle" during which the manager provides a list of key questions the bankers should be asking. Instead of just sending them off into their cubicles to read from a script, the huddle is a time when the bankers are coached through practice calls. A system is provided to help the bankers take notes and capture information. The sales manager monitors the calls, and spends time on the spot—while the experience is fresh in their minds—coaching the bankers discuss these challenges, share best practices, and discuss follow-up strategies.

The Customer Check-In night ends with a group debriefing during which the manager leads a brief Check-in Huddle. Just as the bankers listened to the customers, the manager listens to his or her bankers, because they are the stars of the bank's show.

The sales manager asks his bankers, "Talk about the questions we asked tonight. Which ones worked well and which didn't? What kinds of answers did you get? What needs did the questions uncover? Who wins the prize for asking the most questions? How are you going to follow up on the needs you uncovered?"

> **Without asking one specific sales-related question, the bankers and their sales assistants uncovered more than 200 cross-solving—not cross-selling—opportunities.**

Business bankers can employ a similar approach. One east coast bank ran a Check-in session one morning to ask business clients to describe their experiences with the bank and with their relationship managers. Without asking one specific sales-related question, the bankers and their sales assistants uncovered more than 200 cross-solving opportunities—new initiatives the customers were planning or struggling with that had financial components about which the bank was unaware.

In one morning, for the cost of a few phone calls, that

team of business bankers generated a host of leads that were sitting in their own backyard just waiting for someone to look out the window and notice them. In addition, the bank gathered a fortune's worth of research they could use to map the needs, issues, personal hopes and dreams of their current clients.

Finally, instead of interrupting Jack at home during "Family Guy" with a stale, canned pitch for a commodity product, the team of bankers had parachuted behind the lines into the harried lives of hundreds of business people saying, in effect, "Tell me where it hurts. Tell me about your aspirations and frustrations, what's going on in your corner of the world and in your industry, and what could we be doing to help you and your organization get where you want to go?"

This is Prospecting 101—generating more business from businesses that already have a propensity to buy from your bank. Like Tom Feltenstein's "*Neighborhood Marketing*" concept, technology may appear to drive modern businesses but there is a good reason people still fly halfway around the world just to spend ninety minutes eyeball to eyeball discussing a potential transaction.

The good news is bankers only have to go down the street to find prospects hungry to talk about their businesses. The bad news is most bankers talk too much about themselves and their products, give up too easily and—most importantly—launch the ground war without running the air campaign first.

Air Campaigns, Big and Small

There are many ways to fish where the fish are biting. Some are out of reach of most banks. For the giants in the business—Commerce Bank, Bank of America, Wachovia—it has been to build a branch on every corner—or very nearly. Commerce is credited with being near the top of its class with this strategy, building hundreds of new branches with lots of bright, arresting red details, all-glass fronts, and bright lighting that make the banks feel exciting, open, and inviting, and then hanging huge signs on the front announcing extended hours, and seven-day banking.

This branch-building frenzy began with a conversation that Commerce and other banks had with their customers. The intermediary was the ATM machine, which is great for dispensing cash but does nothing to attract deposits. Bankers who once thought that all banking was going to move online discovered that relying on Internet banking to fill the deposit and product sales gap didn't work. Instead, it gave customers a chance to shop around online and discover that—lo and behold—who needs to park money in a bank when you can earn more in a brokerage cash account or some other short-term solution? Money, by itself, is loyal only to the highest return.

Surveys conducted by the Federal Reserve Board indicate that the single most important factor influencing a customer's choice of banks is the location of the institution's branches.

What was missing was the conversation—the human touch.

The FDIC issued a report on branch banking during the big build-up in branches and concluded that, "despite technological advances that have made it easier to conduct financial services activities without physically entering a bank branch, it seems that banking consumers like the convenience of bank branches. Surveys conducted by the Federal Reserve Board indicate that the single most important factor influencing a customer's choice of banks is the location of the institution's branches.

Branch growth has been successful in spurring deposit growth. Mercer Oliver Wyman, a financial services consulting firm, reported that the number of new bank branches grew an average of 1.3 percent a year between 2000 and 2005 while deposits grew at an average 6.2 percent annual rate. The FDIC reported that the numbers got even better in 2006: branch locations grew by 2.6 percent while total deposits grew by 9 percent.

But bankers have discovered that they cannot thrive on the Starbucks model alone. For one thing, the growth is believed by many experts to be a result of money moving from one bank to another that's more convenient. This is great for building market share, but it has nothing to do with organic growth. It's passive and probably unsustainable. At some point there are too many banks feeding from the same trough. Like any war in history, you can't win by bombs alone.

Another problem is that the boom in branches has caused a shortage of well-trained bankers who are expected to do more than just count currency. Charles H. Wendel, President of Financial Institutions Consulting, observes that,

> "All the training in the world, all the incentives will never turn some staff into salespeople. Management's choice is to continue to invest in lost causes or replace. Remarkably, to this day, too many players avoid this difficult but ultimately very rewarding decision. ... [F]ailing to address the people issue makes sales success highly unlikely."

The human touch, when a person walks into a branch, is an opportunity to talk with a customer about something other than the weather or the price of gasoline. You can't grow a bank by staffing the branches with bodies who are untrained or unskilled in the art of conversation.

The Ground War

Too many business bankers today fail to understand the most basic prospecting concepts that are well-entrenched in other industries. Among the conversations that need to take place before going out to converse with prospects is the one that takes place within the bank:

What kind of business are we looking for?
What are we good at, and how does it compare to market opportunities?
What industries dominate our marketing territory and where are they?
Who are our competitors and what are they doing?
Have we matched our goals to our bank's strategy and vision?

Once this conversation has taken place, the next conversation is about those overlooked backyard opportunities we discussed earlier: how can we leverage the assets we already have?

One of our earliest clients was Jonathan Rohde, senior vice president of the business banking group for a Chicago bank. He has had 160 bankers reporting to him in 26 markets. We have been working with him for fourteen years and his observations are based on years of trial and error, failure and success.

In 1999, Rohde oversaw the implementation of a new database sales management system for his bank's small-business market segment that aimed to help reduce its sales cost and increase account revenues. "It's a rule of thumb in sales organizations like ours that 30 percent of customers account for 70 to 80 percent of profits," he explained. "Our challenge was to use the tool to help us have better conversations with our customers, so more of these accounts will be profitable."

Almost a decade later, Rohde tells us:

> "The quickest way to growth is customers, referral sources, and then prospects. There's no way you can achieve your growth targets without an acquisition strategy.
>
> "One of the tactics we developed was generating leads by association. The best performers with the best growth in new customers were those who leveraged their existing customers to generate referrals that included an introduction.
>
> "If an existing customer feels good about his or her banker, there is a natural desire to help you out. Every business owner is entrepreneurial by nature and shares a goal with the banker—to generate new business. We find that customers who like us want to help our bankers out.
>
> "Sometimes it's as easy as a banker asking a customer for an introduction to one or several of the customer's customers who might benefit from what the bank has to offer. Another approach is to put a list of company names the bank has identified as potential prospects in front of our existing customers to see if they might have a contact with these other business owners.

"This has been a win for us. Out of ten prospects it's not unusual that there is at least one person at one of those companies that our customer knows through golf or some other connection.

"We also find this technique is a great way of testing existing relationships. If a client declines to help our banker, then the banker hasn't connected at the right level. Maybe there's a trust issue. Maybe the client is worried that our banker might pull a fast one behind his or her back.

"The best result is when the client picks up the phone and calls the acquaintance in his network and says, 'I want you to meet my banker. Let's have lunch.'"

Cold Shouldering Cold Calls

Why any sales organization would consider archaic prospecting tactics such as cold calling or even "cold" direct mail is beyond us. Consider some statistics:

Cold call close rates are about 1 percent.

Direct mail response rates have fallen to an all-time low: less than 2 percent.

Conversion rates for a "cold" letter with a phone call follow up are less than 8 percent.

Voice-mail return rates have fallen to about one in twelve, and only one in fifty are returned by the target prospect.

Banker Jonathan Rohde says that instead of cold calling and other "cold" prospecting approaches,

"We spend a lot of time warming the market up through our third-party approaches (referrals by existing customers) and with case studies where we show what we've done to help businesses solve problems. We aren't selling a product but a concept.

"When we introduced remote deposit, the message was built around how remote deposit can get cash to the bank quicker. That's a product pitch wrapped in a warm and fuzzy message. It's not about going out and knocking on doors of office parks.

"We've sliced the market up to identify new opportunities in businesses that we already have knowledge about. I can pick up the phone and make myself busy talking to companies, but they might not be the right companies."

Chapter 4: X Marks the Spot

"The general who wins the battle makes many calculations...before the battle is fought."

—Sun Tzu, Chinese philosopher, 6th Century BC

BETWEEN THE TWO of us we have more than sixty years experience in the banking business and can remember the days when you had to be incompetent or crooked to fail, because the government regulated everything. Deregulation confused bankers who had never needed to compete and many got into trouble. Veterans will never forget the thrift meltdown of the late 1980s.

From a sales perspective, we went from an industry driven by public relations and other forms of soft or passive marketing to having to think and act like true sales professionals: how do we go out and butt heads to get new business? This was a nearly insurmountable task for old-line bankers who'd come up through the ranks operating by ancient rules of behavior that today would be laughable.

Jack recalls as a young banker in the late 1970s going to his president when executives at a competing bank ran into some trouble. "I told him, 'We have a golden opportunity here to attract customers without needing to bash the other guys. A lot of their customers would probably welcome a call from a different bank right about now.'

"I was shocked when he refused to do anything that might even hint at taking advantage of another bank's misfortune. In those days it was considered unsportsmanlike to call on the competition's customers, under any circumstances."

To put the banking industry's archaic mind-set in perspective, during the same period that Jack's bank president was ignoring the chance to lure business from a vulnerable competitor, a tiny telephone company called MCI Communications was on the verge of winning an epic anti-trust suit against AT&T, forcing the break-up of another highly-regulated mega-industry: Ma Bell.

Most bankers at the time had no idea how to make business development calls and those who tried pounding the pavement often came back empty-handed. Business banking meant glad-handing at the chamber of commerce, being on the board of service clubs, and rounds of golf at the country club. So long as you did nothing immoral or illegal, it was presumed you had a job for life. Bankers rarely quit to go work for another bank, except to get a better title and a higher salary.

So long as you did nothing immoral or illegal, it was presumed you had a job for life. Bankers rarely quit to go work for another bank, except to get a better title and a higher salary.

Today, loyalty extends only as far as your latest results and competition is fierce from all quarters. Bankers have only recently learned the value of strategic and tactical planning, and how to identify those segments of their markets most likely to yield the most efficient return in sales and profits.

Drawing A Bead

Among the many conversations that we recommend take place before a banker ever talks to a prospect begins with internal market research. You can be a great salesperson who has all the skills and tools to get the job done but if you're prospecting in the wrong places, you're going to be wasting your time or producing sub-par results.

Park National Bank uses the term "wheelhouse" to explain the concept governing how it identifies the bank's most promising prospects.

Target markets are evaluated by several basic measurements, including:

A bank's particular expertise or experience in specific industries.

The financial needs and concerns of both the bank and its prospects.

We encourage bankers to mine the information they already have to help identify where their best opportunities lie. Questions to be answered include:

- Which clients are in your wheelhouse?
- What have they purchased from you recently and what do these ideal clients have in common?
- Is there a theme that could guide you to prospects with similar habits or characteristics that are in similar industries?
- Why have clients bought, what benefits did they want, and what were their goals?
- Where are your current clients located?
- What are your clients' professional interests, affiliations, and reading habits?
- What are their buying cycles and habits?
- What motivates clients to buy from your bank, and what causes them to choose the other guys?
- What are the trends in your clients' industries, how do companies differentiate themselves, and who are their principal competitors?

These are the same questions anyone in any business asks, or should ask, before they embark on a sales career. Banks have many advantages lacking in most other industries: you already know quite a lot about customer's spending habits, cash flow, seasonal rhythms, location, and—thanks to improved data mining—you can also determine which customers in which industries fall into that 30 percent that generate the lion's share of profits.

Read It and Reap

We've established some basic truths about prospecting in the banking industry:

- Cold calling is an ineffective, self-defeating waste of time.
- Sales blitzes are also an ineffective, self-defeating waste of time.
- Bankers need to think like their customers, who are by definition entrepreneurs. How does banker-preneur sound?
- Your best customers can be your most powerful prospecting tool.
- There is tremendous opportunity for traditional banks in the wake of the 2007 credit crisis. Expect a back-to-basics, FDIC-focused movement.
- "Pinging" and touches with value create a bond between banker and prospect
- Prospecting is like chess: the winner is the one who anticipates the anticipations of others.
- Business in the new millennium may be increasingly facilitated and accelerated by technology, but in the end, it's still the "fit" that defines profitable, long-term relationships.
- A solid partnership begins and is sustained by a conversation focused on the prospect as opposed to on the bank or on its products.
- A performance culture built on trust always outperforms a sales culture built on product pushing and tick marks.

Once you've had all these conversations within the bank—between leaders and relationship managers, with your existing customers, and with yourself about your individual competencies—it's time to find out where the fish are schooling.

What's In It For Them?

As we previously noted, the typical business owner or decision-maker spends 95 percent of his or her time on everything except vendors. Within that remaining five percent, unless there is a pressing need, bankers will likely rank far down the priority list, behind suppliers of raw materials or inventory, business management and communications systems and equipment, marketing, maintenance, transportation, real estate, accounting and legal—just to name a few.

We've also established that banking services, like medical care, is a need for which we rarely shop, even when there is a pressing need. Both, incorrectly, are viewed as commodities. When was the last time you compared your local hospital's inpatient mortality rate to those of other hospitals in your area? How many of us actually check the relative ranking of the medical school where our doctors got their training?

Shopping for a bank is similarly daunting, time-consuming, and imprecise. It entails having to explain your business, disclose information to people you don't know well enough to trust, and may communicate desperation. This is more than an imaginary concern. As Park National's Tom Doherty notes: "If one of our managers leaves a voice mail for a business owner and the owner calls right back saying, 'Can you come out right away?' I want to run the other direction. That's probably going to be the person who's overdrawn and desperate for a loan."

Instead, the prospects worth pursuing are those hardest to reach, whose five percent of vendor time is over-booked. The way around this is to hang up your banker hat and think like a prospect. If you've gone through all the hoops so far and identified a prospect in the trucking industry, for example, you should know enough about the latest trends in the trucking industry before you make your initial contact.

The prospects worth pursuing are those hardest to reach, whose five percent of vendor time is over-booked. The way around this is to put away your banker hat and think like a prospect.

You could spend a lot of time boning up on the trucking business through trade journals and online research. Happily, there are services that do this for you, aggregating articles, commentary, and analysis on all major industries. The leading firm specifically serving the banking industry is Raleigh, North Carolina-based First Research, Inc., cofounded by a former banker—Bobby Martin—who was inspired in part by America's first great salesman, John Henry Patterson, founder of National Cash Register in the 1880s.

Patterson was a coal industry executive when he bought a company that made cash registers. Sales limped along for about a decade until, so the legend goes, he met Thomas Watson Sr., a butcher who owned one of Patterson's registers. Watson is said to have told Patterson the reason he wasn't selling more machines is he wasn't listening to what customers wanted, and then delivering it.

Watson joined Patterson's company and helped put it on the map. Patterson began to make some money when he created a sales process, became a wealthy man when NCR went public, and Watson went on to become an even wealthier man after he went off and started his own company—the predecessor to IBM.

First Research – The Linchpin to TAPS

A variety of sizes of banks have employed TAPS successfully. They range in size from community banks to regional players to two of the top five. The banks are geographically dispersed and their markets are diverse. The one thing they all have in common is that they have seamlessly integrated First Research into the process.

Bobby Martin's First Research story is worth telling because it is, in a way, the story of banking's evolution from quasi-government agency to free-market competitor. Bobby was a business banker in North Carolina calling on the CFOs of mid-sized companies in his market. Like most bankers, his prospecting conversations were largely focused on what the bank had to offer. He had little knowledge and not much to offer about the specifics of the prospect's needs and industry trends.

> "I was calling on an engineering company one day and the CFO was patiently explaining to me how her industry worked—the four or five types of engineering, what percentage of revenue went to payroll, and so on. I commented to her that it would be a lot better if I knew all this before I went out to see her. She agreed and we chatted about this for a bit. An idea began to form in my head.
>
> "An auto parts manufacturer was moving into town and I got an appointment to make a presentation to the CEO. This time, I did a lot of

research first. I centered my presentation around the company's industry and their business, talking about the need to structure their lines of credit around revenue cycles that I had learned about ahead of time. The CEO chose my bank because of the knowledge we displayed about the auto parts industry.

"I tried the same thing with an oil distribution company, and it worked. They told me I was the first banker who understood their business. I was on a roll.

"It was clear that when I knew what kept prospects and customers awake at night, and really understood the nuances of their banking needs, I had something valuable and unique to offer that set me apart from the competition.

"When I knew what kept prospects and customers awake at night, and really understood the nuances of their banking needs, I had something valuable and unique to offer that set me apart from the competition."

"This was before the Internet became so sophisticated and it was not as easy to find up-to-date, useful information. The bank had a research department but it took a week to get what I needed and it was often incomplete or written from the perspective of an investor. So I started making information cheat sheets where I kept a record of everything I learned by reading periodicals, from the research department, gossip, and so on.

"The cheat sheets became my essential tool in preparing for my first conversation with prospects.

> I could say with confidence, 'I've been keeping up with your industry and I'll save you the time of having to explain the history of your world.' I could demonstrate by my knowledge that I cared about their business and often discovered that I had a perspective or a bit of knowledge they found useful.
>
> "Then I decided it would be great to have all my cheat sheets available on a computer. Everything came together when I teamed up with a research expert, Ingo Winzer, and quit banking to start First Research. We put together packages of industry intelligence written so that prospecting bankers could quickly understand and use it to help their customers.
>
> "Today First Research is a fine-tuned system of gathering, analyzing, and distilling information on about seven hundred industry segments, updated quarterly, provided in such a way that it only takes a few minutes to do what used to take me hours and hours. We've even gone on to podcasting reports that bankers can listen to in their cars on the way to meetings with prospects."

Martin says, "Prospecting is like dating. You don't make much of an impression talking about yourself throughout dinner. What counts is how well you listen and understand."

Incredibly, Martin reports that only about a third of First Research's 400-plus clients make full use of the service. A third never use it and a third use it now and again. "For some organizations it's like a gym membership. It makes them feel good but it doesn't do any good unless you use it."

The ideas and concepts we've discussed so far have all been about the conversations that take place before you've placed the first phone call or written the first letter. Now it's time to put all this knowledge to work in a prospecting system.

PART II
The Trusted Advisor Prospecting System

Chapter 5: The Magic Touch

"There is only one boss. The customer. And he can fire everybody...from the chairman on down, simply by spending his money somewhere else."

—Sam Walton, founder of Wal-Mart

ACCORDING TO recent surveys, banks are making some headway in improving their image among business customers, but there is still a long way to go. In 2006, the industry earned the highest mark ever in the University of Michigan's Customer Satisfaction Index. Still, banks ranked below life-insurance companies.

Bank executives and managers who persist in focusing on product lines, silos, quotas, and other traditional approaches to sales are ignoring the fundamentals of human behavior. Instead of pushing, they should be pulling. A 2007 J.D. Power survey found that a five-percentage-point increase in the number of a bank's customers who count themselves "highly" committed to banking with

There is plenty of rain being made in financial services, but there are a lot more buckets trying to catch it.

the firm—instead of just "moderately"—translated into a $1 billion boost in deposits per million customers.

A five percent increase in customer satisfaction may sound modest, but bank managers know how hard it is to budge the needle in a highly competitive business where sophisticated rivals are coming at you from all sides, selling the same commodities you are, to a crowd of informed prospects. Imagine owning a gas station that shares a busy intersection with three other gas stations, and everybody's selling at the same price. That's essentially the struggle facing our industry in the new millennium. There is plenty of rain being made in financial services, but there are a lot more buckets trying to catch it.

We've made progress, but too much of what is being done is cosmetic, trendy, or incomplete. We call our sales people relationship managers, and banks are investing more in training than ever before. But most banks are still catching up to the rest of the business world, and most relationship managers aren't being coached in the art of building lasting, profitable relationships.

When we started our financial services marketing careers, the big concerns were making sure there were enough dog biscuits at the drive-in window, plenty of toasters on hand for the premium promotion, and that each local charity that asked for a donation got the same amount.

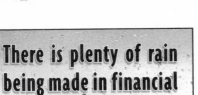

Today the responsibilities of the banking professional are rigorous and complex. Marketing and sales must be connected at the customer experience and the wallet. To create "highly" committed customers, banks need to be highly committed to changing culture, choosing performance over obedience.

In another book in this series we address the problems faced by bank managers and executives in creating an atmosphere and a framework that supports and encourages relationship managers to focus on developing long-term conversations with customers. In these pages, we want to show you how to start a conversation with someone you've never met—a prospect.

Sourcing for Dollars

In the past, banks had to rely for lead ideas on the phone book and credit reports on companies in their markets. Today, bankers can do a great deal of sourcing using the Internet without leaving their desks.

Here are a few ideas we suggest for gathering sources that can be turned into potential prospects through the TAPS system.

> ***Be an incessant reader:*** Local and national newspapers, business publications, online business news sites, economic reports, investment trend reports, and other media outlets may mention specific companies or industries that fit your profile of best prospects. Crain Communications Inc. publishes weekly magazines in major markets (e.g., *Crain's Chicago)* and trade journals covering industries as diverse as plastics and waste management. These publications report on executive changes, business expansions, industry trends, and much more. Even advertising can tell you something about what's happening in specific industries.

Become a relentless observer. Savvy sales bankers are always on the prowl, even on their way to and from work. They use cell phone cameras to capture information on trucks at stop lights and carry digital tape recorders to capture information they can research later.

Become a relentless observer. Savvy sales bankers are always on the prowl, even on their way to and from work.

Your marketing department can buy lists from InfoUSA, IDEXEC.com, or any number of other data aggregators that can help shave time off your sourcing clock.

Read the want ads every Sunday. Look for openings for CFOs, treasurers, senior managers and so on at the kinds of companies that fit your prospect profile. People in motion (PIM) creates money in motion (MIM).

Check out hotel and conference centers. Businesses are always holding meetings and seminars and it's a good opportunity to collect valuable information and learn about trends in industries in your market area. You might be surprised what you find, as Bob St. Meyer demonstrated to a roomful of bankers he was teaching at a hotel in Michigan.

The bank that had retained us wanted to focus on prospecting among trade associations because of the deposit opportunities they offered. Bob happened to notice on the meeting announcement monitor in the hallway that two trade associations were meeting in the same hotel that day.

At the end of his training session, he asked the bankers if they knew what other meetings were taking place at the hotel. Not one banker had noticed that two prospects were meeting yards away from where they had been sitting for six hours.

Not one banker had noticed that two prospects were meeting yards away from where they had been sitting all day.

Seek out speaking engagements. We find there is great interest within business communities to hear from bankers. We speak at every banking conference, banking school, and state association meeting we can find. As a banker you will be received as an expert and if you have something to say of value, you'll usually walk away from every program with a handful of leads. If you are uncomfortable speaking in front of an audience and don't want to take a course in public speaking, demonstrate your expertise by writing an article for the Chamber of Commerce newsletter or the Rotary Gazette.

Mine the Internet. We're big fans of Google News Alerts. This free service allows sales associates to create a dynamic list of people, businesses, industries, and to have news sent to them automatically about specific industries. There are many other web-based lead sources, including Yahoo Yellow Pages, Sorkins, and Switchboard.com.

First Impressions

Before a banker begins the TAPS process or sends out the first letter to a prospect, or drops off information to the prospect's place of business, he or she needs to make sure it's going to the right person. You may have done all your research, checked the company's web site, and done all your due diligence. But it helps to double check your advance work with the gatekeeper.

Gatekeepers are too often perceived as the enemy of sales, a moat between you and the prospect that you have to connive to get around. There are still workshops being taught about how to "get around" the gatekeeper. But creating an adverserial relationship with gatekeepers can be frustrating, and trying to sneak past can be both embarrassing and destructive. In fact, gatekeepers can be allies if the relationship is viewed as a potential collaboration instead of as combat.

Gatekeeer Tips

The first step is to treat the gatekeeper with respect and honesty:

Learn and use their name.

Identify yourself, your job, and your affiliation.

Ask for their help. (You may be surprised how helpful people are willing to be when they are asked.)

Explain your purpose, phrasing it as a benefit. For example, "We're updating our list for people that may want to receive our monthly economic update," or, "I've uncovered three best practices about your industry that might help add to your bottom line," or, if appropriate, "Our bank offers financial workshops from time to time and I wanted to make sure the correct person receives an invitation."

Ask for the contact information you need and be sure to record the gatekeeper's information, including name, title, email, and so on. Respect resistance. If the gate-keeper doesn't want to give out information, ask if the information can be sent to the gatekeeper and how best to send it (regular mail or email).

Sometimes it makes sense, if you're already in the neighborhood, to drop in on a potential prospect and get or confirm the information you need in person. This is NOT a cold call. It is a recon mission.

Ask the receptionist or other gatekeeper for help and gather the information you need, just as you would by phone.

Make sure to find out if there is more than one person who handles the company's financial affairs, gather business cards, and any other contact information that may be helpful. While you are there, pick up a brochure about the business and scan the office for any trade publications that might be laying around.

Getting Letter Perfect

Your first TAPS impression with a prospect is going to be in writing and that first letter is more successful in opening doors when it focuses on the prospect, not the bank. You'll only get a few seconds to make an impact. Otherwise it'll end up in the recycling bin.

Your letter should generate curiosity, convey valuable information, and create an expectation of future correspondence and a phone call to obtain a face-to-face appointment.

Letter Writing Tips

- Make it about them, not you.
- Start with a strong salutation.
- Keep it simple: a single, coherent thought.
- Get to the point.
- Use boldface type and bullets to draw the eye down the page to the key points.
- Keep the letter to one page.
- Use a creative signoff.
- Suggest your next steps with a post script note.

We've discovered (as you'll notice at the start of each chapter) that you make a strong first impression with an inspirational quote at the top of your letter. Strive to find quotations that have not been over-used, which mean something to the reader, and which create continuity with the purpose and destination of your message. "Big things come in small packages" is a hackneyed phrase that will impress no one. And trying to be too cute can suggest impertinence: "I'm 200 percent against inflation."

The best inspirational quotes convey thoughtfulness, are NOT focused on you or your bank, and express basic truths with great power through colorful, well-chosen language. It's best to give a source for the quote if you have one. We've left them off here for convenience. Some good quotations:

"A diamond is a lump of coal that stuck to its job."

"Never tell anyone what you are going to do until you've done it."

"A turtle doesn't move until it sticks its neck out."

"The difference between a batting record of .250 and .350 is a quarter-inch."

"Success comes not from holding a good hand but playing a poor one well."

There are many good books and even more web sites that offer inspirational quotes organized by subject, or by author. One of the better books is Joe Griffith's *"Speaker's Library of Business Stories, Anecdotes, and Humor."* You can Google "business quotes" or go to sites such as motivationalquotes.com or brainyquote.com. A great quotation can leave such a strong impression that we know of prospects who have lifted them from prospect letters and had them reproduced and distributed around their offices for all to see.

A great quotation can leave such a strong impression that we know of prospects who have lifted them from prospect letters, had them reproduced, and distributed them around their offices for all to see.

We're avid readers of business books and using a quote from a new book is often impressive. You might even conclude your letter by suggesting that you will bring your prospect a copy of the book when you meet.

It's important to choose quotations that won't inadvertently offend or come across as too cynical, presumptuous, or flippant. Avoid quotations that are specific to an ethnic group or religious affiliation. These may seem like obvious pitfalls, but we sometimes forget that we live in a very diverse culture, both as to heritage and politics. If you're going to quote a president, better one that's long gone than one that's still around or the subject of controversy.

The characteristics of a strong letter:

A personal salutation, but not the typical Dear Sir or Dear Madam, or To Whom It May Concern.

A short, declarative first sentence can link to the quote and target the industry. Remember that you're supposed to have done all the research we described in Part One and at the beginning of this chapter before you write the first word.

You aren't writing to a stranger. You're writing to someone about whose business you know more than the prospect will expect, especially in a banker. ("For the past 20 years your customers have gotten used to MedTestCo putting its neck, heart, and soul into keeping up with the rapid technological developments in the medical testing equipment business, and consistently meeting and exceeding their expectations.") Be creative, be specific, but above all be sincere.

Paragraphs should be short and their first lines indented. The most successful letters have one opening paragraph and one closing paragraph. People read the way they eat, in bites. Long, wordy sentences and blocks of type are difficult to consume in the few seconds you have to get attention.

Include up to five bullet points in boldface type. These are either high impact questions or key statements that relate directly to the industry. First Research profiles can be of great assistance here.

Ask yourself, "What's in it for the prospect?" What might be keeping him or her awake at night? Are raw materials or employment costs rising? Is the business tied to the economy in some meaningful way? Is there a seasonal aspect you could address?

Create curiosity. Hold back on your temptation to "pitch" the bank or its products, but do suggest that you may have something of value to offer, such as information about best practices, a free seminar, or some other resource to help their business grow more profitable.

Bring it home. The final paragraph of your letter brings your message together. Make reference to the quote and begin to suggest the action you plan to take as a next step. Keep it short—two or three sentences.

The postscript (P.S.) is a key to getting the appointment. This puts the prospect on notice that you will be following up first by sending him or her some useful information, perhaps an industry report or some other printed material that is NOT about selling products but focused on the prospect's business. Let them know to "expect a call from me on Tuesday, X date at X time." The time is critical. Make it unique. Collaborating with the gatekeeper is great if you can but avoiding them is better and your chances of doing that improve if you will call before 8 o'clock or after 5 o'clock.

Check and re-check grammar, spelling, and so on. Nothing undermines credibility faster than misspelling the name of the company or the person you're writing to. Sloppiness will send your letter straight to recycling.

Do NOT include your business card with your letter: That makes it too easy for the business owner to call and reject you.

Hand-address the bank's envelope and, if available, use an oversized envelope so the letter need not be folded. People open hand-addressed envelopes from banks because it suggests official business, and they tend to open large envelopes because they suggest important documents are inside.

Use interesting stamps instead of the bank's postage meter. It adds a personal touch.

Send no more than five letters a week. Most prospecting systems overlook how busy most bankers are. In addition to the TAPS process, there is networthing, centers of influence, and internal referrals to be tended to. Avoid falling into the trap of falling behind and trying to make up by sending 10 letters one week to make up for a missed week. This interrupts the rhythm and discipline of the process.

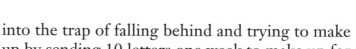

There are many books and online resources to tap into if you feel insecure or uncertain of your writing ability, or want to learn some of the many techniques for creating a winning first letter. Many people are intimidated by a blank page. These letters are so important that you may want to hire a freelancer with experience writing marketing and pitch letters to coach you, or even ghostwrite your letters for you.

On the next page is an example of a TAPS letter our clients have found effective.

March 3, 2008 (or any Monday)

"It is the relationship itself—an interlocking web of personal commitments, over time, based on respect—that is the source of all value."

Charles H. Green
Author, "Trust-Based Selling

Mr. George Costanza
President
Van Dalay Industries
1598 W. Main Street
Anytown, USA 12345

It boils down to trust, George…

Customers and suppliers rely on your staff to exceed expectations day after day. It is that reputation for integrity that has caused me to reach out. Imagine 2008 is a record year at **Van Dalay Industries**. It's likely you:

- **Effectively managed the cash that flowed through your operation**
- **Broadened your product mix and expanded your customer base**
- **Created strategies to protect tangible and intangible business assets**
- **Planned how to replicate your success in 2007**

Helping entrepreneurs achieve their objectives is out of the ordinary for some. At National Bank, collaboration is a way life. You select your attorney, accountant, and other trusted advisors based on "fit" – that intangible connection that extends beyond products and price. All I ask is the opportunity to learn if that "fit" exists between your needs and our solutions. Agree to an initial conversation and I'll bring ***Power Resources***—a list of best in class business books like *Trust-Based Selling*.

Make today and every day a Best Seller!

Jerry Seinfeld

Jerry Seinfeld
Business Development Officer

P.S. Watch for an e-mail/note this week containing some trends about your industry and a expect telephone call from me on **(DATE)** at **(TIME)** to schedule an appointment. If that won't work, simply reply to my correspondence and we'll reschedule.

The Value Touch—Notes and Emails

On Monday, your five TAPS letters to targeted prospects leave the office in personalized, stamped envelopes. That same week the prospect receives another touch—a value touch with a brief note that includes an article or a white paper the prospect may find interesting.

(At the end of this chapter you will find a calendar depicting the TAPS prospecting cycle.)

If you choose to send a note, do that on Wednesday. The goal is to have the prospect receive two touches from you in the same week. That helps to build your personal brand. Emails are sent on Fridays of that first week since it is more immediate.

The goal is to have the prospect receive two touches from you in the same week. That helps to build your personal brand.

Depending on how receptive your prospect is, this could be the beginning of a long correspondence that may or may not end in a sale, but is the way to build a relationship based on mutual interest and trust. Remember that the most successful wealth managers are those who communicated with clients fifteen times a year.

Email can be tricky. Check with your bank on its policies regarding outbound email, make sure you aren't violating any regulations regarding spam, and in any case you should purchase a book or two on effective emails. One we like is "Send: The Essential Guide to Email for Office and Home," by David Shipley and Will Schwalbe.

The key to getting the e-mail opened is the subject line. It is your e-mail envelope. The subject must be compelling and factual to get prospects to open them. If you're writing to MedTestCo, and you're sending some First Research information, or a link to a news article, it'll grab attention if the subject line is specific, such as: "Three testing equipment best practices."

First Research has a chapter in each profile called Recent Developments containing three current articles from reliable news outlets about the industry you are prospecting to. Using this approach makes sending notes and emails easier and adds great value to the recipient.

Remember, it's still about the prospect, not about the bank. How you choose to make this second touch depends on what you learned, in part, from the gatekeeper (does the prospect use email and, if so, will it be provided to you?), and your own style as a sales professional. There are pluses and minuses to both methods. Notes are easy and quick but do require several extra steps. Email is quick but with many security filters in place now, many times you don't know if the email ever got through, and email is increasingly seen as a source of wasted time by many executives. Once again, this may be a task with which some will want professional writing help.

It is important to include all your contact information—phone, fax, bank website; an "opt-out" disclaimer; and any other information and notices that your bank or the law requires.

Sample Email or Note:

To: ethan.allen@furnishings.com
From: betty.jones@nationalbank.com
Subject: Three Trends in Furniture Manufacturing

Good Day Ethan:

Furnishing Industries has continually set the customer experience standard in the furniture industry. Maybe these ideas can help your next-level strategies. I'll bring some additional data when we meet.

Automation Improvements—Newer computer-controlled machinery and automation processes can produce further efficiencies in an industry that, until recently, made almost everything by hand. Capital investment in this industry is still very low. Computer-aided design (CAD) use and mass production in large companies is evidence of increased automation. Broyhill, a unit of Furniture Brands International, pioneered mass-production techniques.

Direct Internet Ordering—Small manufacturers can expand sales to retailers and directly to the public using the Internet. Because 80 percent of customers dislike furniture shopping, a comprehensive product catalog online can help manufacturers meet consumer needs. Industry observers predict that furniture sellers will have a tough time on the Web due to high costs associated with shipping and returns.

Plant Improvements—Many furniture manufacturers are restructuring their plant floors to create "cells" or "plants within a plant" that make specific parts or products. This job-shop workflow allows for better inventory, quality control, and production flexibility. Self- managed teams take care of quality, production control, and machine setup.

I'll reach out, as promised, on (Date/Time) to schedule our initial appointment. If you would rather call me to schedule a time that works best for you, I'll be in the office Friday from 10:00–11:30 AM and 3:30–5:30 PM. I can also be reached Monday from 7:30 AM to 10:00 AM.

To great conversations and to your continued success!

Signature
Contact Info.

The Trusted Advisor Prospecting System (TAPS) Cycle

Each Cycle Starts on Monday With Five Letters...

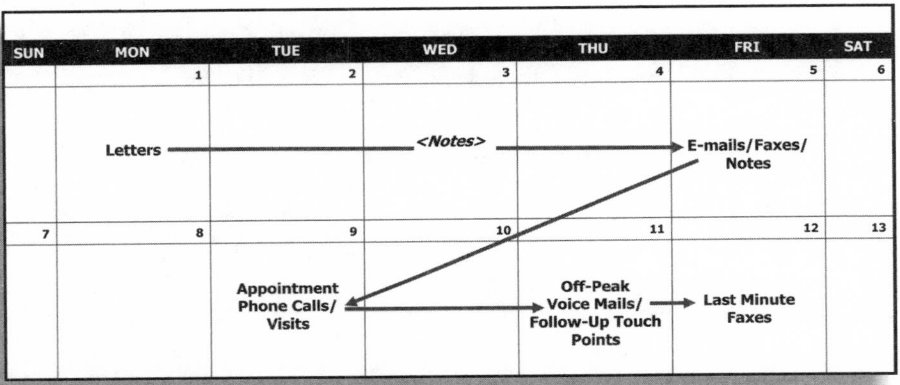

And Repeats Throughout The Month.

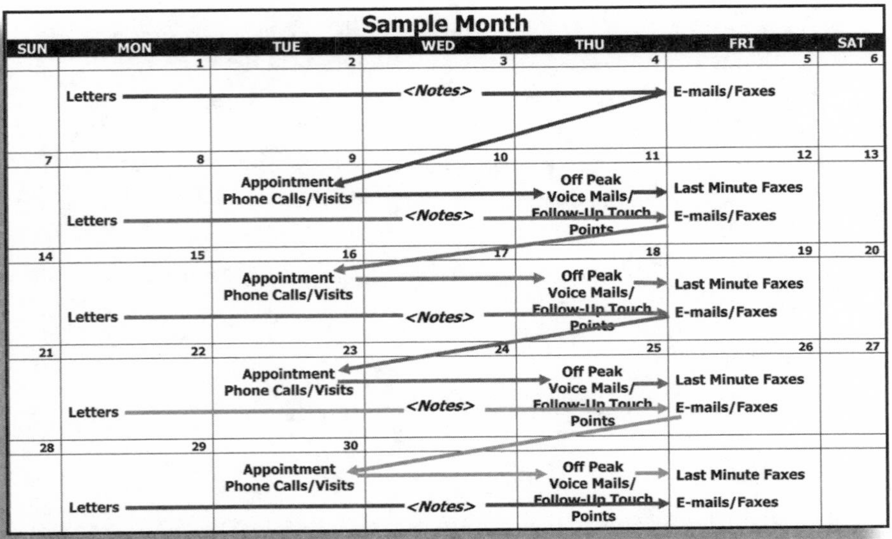

Chapter 6: Phoning It Out

"If email had been around before the telephone was invented, people would have said, 'Forget email. With this new telephone invention I can actually talk to people!' "

—Source Unknown

YOUR TAILORED LETTER, the value-added email or note, and the research about your prospect have laid the groundwork for the next step: asking for an appointment.

Your prospects are as busy and harried as you. To manage time efficiently, some bankers using TAPS try to make initial appointment calls for all prospects in one sitting, on Tuesday of each week. This keeps the rest of the week open for your other responsibilities and for second and third phone calls to prospects who haven't responded.

Some choose to make two calls Tuesday morning and three calls Tuesday evening. Some make three calls on Tuesday and two on Wednesday. Whatever approach you take, expect and allow time for phone tag and other complications.

Always call at the time suggested. We've had numerous examples of bankers missing a call by a minute or two and the prospect tells them that they were two minutes late for their "appointment."

Key steps to appointment success include:

Do a pre-call call. This is a call at an off hour to the direct phone number of the decision maker, when they will likely be out of the office. The goal? To *listen* to their voice mail. Do NOT leave a message. Are they fast-paced or more deliberate? Do they sound friendly or abrupt? Do they record their own voice mail message? Everything is a clue to how to approach this prospect.

Prepare and practice a 30-second to two-minute conversation. If you reach the prospect the first time, what you say in the first few seconds is critical.

Have all your research and correspondence in front of you, and the prospect company's website on your monitor. Review the big picture pages, such as "About", "Our Staff", "In the News", and so on. None of this should take more than a couple of minutes and you should be ready in case you get right through to your prospect.

Remember, you are NOT selling anything. You are, in effect, checking in on a new relationship, continuing a conversation that, while one-sided thus far, you have already started. But in this conversation you are talking not about yourself but about the prospect, and what matters most to him or her.

Stand to make the call. This stretches your diaphragm, helps calm your nerves, and creates a stronger, more dynamic sound.

Do NOT begin with "How are you?" unless your prospect happens to be your Uncle Pete. It is possibly the most insincere and inappropriate thing you can say to someone to whom you are an unfamiliar, faceless voice on the phone, an uninvited distraction from the chores that take up 95 percent of his or her time.

Do NOT read from a script. Write a few bullet points and practice before you dial, and try it out on your sales manager to make sure you're fully prepared.

Prepare ahead of time the message you want to leave if you reach the gatekeeper or voice mail. If you've stated a time you will call in your previous email or note, keep the date and time. You'll be amazed how impressive that is to a prospect. It shows respect and responsibility. It also subtly shifts the balance of power—you kept your word, now the prospect feels slightly challenged to show his or her respect for that.

The Dating Game

The Trusted Advisor Prospecting System avoids scripting and encourages creativity through the use of value-focused touch points and pings. Bankers who successfully develop a process that fits their style soon become naturals at making these calls, and the results show it.

Because these are not sales calls, cold or otherwise, the banker is relieved of the pressure to produce an instant result. That's why this dating game is such a challenge to so many banks. It's not that they dispute the concepts of TAPS. In fact, when we lead this in a one-day workshop version, many bankers say they have done parts of TAPS for a long time. Few bankers put it all together, however, and fewer make it part of their sales DNA.

The problem is that culture in banks changes slowly. For prospecting to work, bank managers have to be enthusiastically behind it, and in it for the long haul. That's where the payoff comes. It's all in how the manager coaches the process. Efficient performance instead of obedience to quotas and tick marks helps build trust with clients and generates sustainable revenues.

A few tips for when you reach the decision-maker:

•**Use the prospect's name.**

•**Thank them for taking your call** and immediately ask if this is a BAD time to chat. It's a terrible first impression for a prospect to have to cut you off in the middle of a sentence because he's in a meeting. If it is a bad time, ask when a better time would be

•**Get to the point.** Without mentioning the letter, you want to discover how the prospect stays current with trends and best practices in his or her industry.

•**Look for the opening to transition to the appointment.** "I have found three trends in a new white paper about commercial printing you may find interesting and I'm curious if you might have some time next *(day of the week)* for an initial conversation."

•**If you get the date, confirm it** and wrap up the call. Don't get drawn into conducting the appointment at this stage. If the conversation is getting too deep, look for a "communications hook" to move the conversation to the appointment.

This is another area where there are plenty of resources for picking up telephone techniques but you'll learn the most by doing it. Each time you have a conversation like this, you'll figure out what works and what doesn't, and how to read people who are disengaged and should be called again another time.

Sample Phone Calls

EXAMPLE #1: *Appointment Conversation*

Prospect: This is Bob Johnson.

RM: Hello Bob. This is Betty Jones. I'm a relationship manager with National Bank over on Fourth Street, less than a mile from your office. Thank you for taking my call. Is this a bad time to chat for a couple of minutes?

Prospect: I have a few minutes.

RM: Thanks. In the past twelve months three of my clients in the manufacturing area have achieved record revenues by focusing on some key issues. What are two or three issues that are facing your company?

Prospect: Expanding revenue is one of our goals, of course, but every company strives for that. How does a bank help with that?

RM: Technology for example. It's not the bank's but helping clients understand which technology is a fad and which is a trend.

Prospect: It's interesting you mention technology. That very subject came up earlier this week with my business partner.

RM: I'm not surprised. My clients tell me advances in production equipment and project management software are helping them isolate costs and prevent overruns—protecting profit margins. If you'd like some specifics, I'd like to stop by and discuss a best practice or two. Would Tuesday morning be a good time to meet?

Prospect: It would have to be early in the morning and I wouldn't be able to give you much time.

RM: How early are you in?

Prospect: I usually arrive by 7:30.

RM: That will be great. How much time can you share, and who else will be at the meeting?

Prospect: Only an hour and probably just me at this point.

RM: That's perfect. See you next Tuesday morning in your office at (confirm address) at 7:30. Thanks for your time today.

EXAMPLE #2: *Appointment Conversation*

This is the same opening as the first example, but instead of "Is this a bad time to chat?" try, "Is this a bad time for me to add some value to your business?"

Prospect: What? That's a new one.

RM: I'm not surprised. People don't often think of bankers as performance consultants. As an example, how do you stay current with trends and best practices in your industry?

Prospect: Publications, conferences, word of mouth. The usual.

RM: Interesting you didn't mention your banker. I see my responsibility as a relationship manager from several perspectives. One is to put buyers and sellers together. Another is to provide our clients with timely, relevant industry information that helps them grow to the next-level.

Prospect: Don't you make loans at your bank?

RM: We do lots of things, but I don't know how we can help unless I understand the issues that are driving your business and industry today, and into the future. Would Tuesday morning be a good time for us to get together to discuss these?

Prospect: It would have to be early in the morning and I wouldn't be able to give you much time.

RM: How early are you in?

Prospect: I usually arrive by 7:30.

RM: That will be great. How much time can you share with me, and who else will be at the meeting?

Prospect: Only an hour and probably just me. But I'm not looking to change banks.

RM: That's perfect. See you next Tuesday morning in your office at (confirm address) at 7:30. And, I'll bring some trend-based information about your industry. The conversation I hope to have is about changing your business for the better.

If the prospect mentions your letter, you have a good shot at getting the appointment. Here's an actual TAPS conversation Jack heard while coaching a banker:

Prospect: Are you that banker who sent me the letter?

Banker: Yes I am. What were your thoughts?

Prospect: It was different.

Banker: How so?

Prospect: It didn't mention anything about the bank or your products. It was mostly about us.

Banker: That's the approach we like to take at National Bank. Can we continue this conversation in your office?

Prospect: Okay, but I'm not changing banks.

Banker: I understand. Remember in the letter I mentioned a white paper about your industry? I'll bring it along. What day and time works best for you?

Speaking and Standing Out

When you make that call you promised or planned at 7:47 in the morning, or after hours, and the gatekeeper answers, the less you tell them, and the more you do that pleasantly, the better your chances. Your letter promised you would call at a specific time so you can truthfully tell the gatekeeper, "Ms. Smith is expecting my call."

If the gatekeeper wants to know more, successful TAPS bankers suggest, "It is about the white paper I promised to bring to Ms. Smith about improving efficiency through robotics." If the gatekeeper has to take a message or put you into voice mail, first try to obtain any information you don't have, such as email address, direct phone number, and so on. DO NOT manipulate the gatekeeper, and don't press to be put through to the prospect by suggesting you are "following up on my letter."

Voice mail is rarely returned in business because most sales people are poorly trained. The message you leave on a prospect's voice mail must be BIG—Brief, Interesting, and Gone.

Keep it under 20 seconds in length. Touch on themes mentioned in your letter or email/note, without specifically mentioning the letter or email/note. At the end, leave your name, bank affiliation, and phone number (say it clearly and slowly).

Sample voice mail messages that were returned.

(All begin with a salutation: Mr. Smith or Ms. Jones)

- "A medical practice I partner with has improved cash flow by 18%. If bottom line results are of interest in your practice, call me, Melissa Johnson, National Bank, 555-122-1212."

- "I've come across three new best practices for minimizing restaurant inventory shrinkage. If you would like a copy of them call me, Melissa Johnson, National Bank, 555-122-1212."

- "I was on Route 95 this morning behind one of your drivers and I wanted to compliment your driver. For more specifics, call me, Melissa Johnson, National Bank, 555-122-1212."

- "If you are like most business owners today, you tend to sleep like a baby…wake up every two hours and cry. If you would like to cry less and sleep better, call me, Melissa Johnson, National Bank, 555-122-1212."

Some are direct, some are creative. All are refreshing and will be remembered in a sea of sales pablum in which your prospect has heard every attempt by a banker to get in the door using products or a come-on like, "I would like to show you how we could save you some money."

"This just isn't me," you say? The point of TAPS is to shift the focus away from you and to the prospect. We know this works in spite of how awkward these messages may seem to you right now. We've helped bankers get appointment rates as high as 80%. What's your score now?

A Marathon, Not a Sprint

This is not a book just about writing letters or making phone calls. The details of setting up a system for institutionalizing this process and managing it well are far more complex than would fit in one book. But it must be said that prospecting, when done correctly, is a series of conversations during which trust is built, value is identified, and relationships become cemented.

For those who adopt this systematic and patient approach, being the fourth gas station on the busy corner becomes a non-issue, because most of the competition is still out there pushing product and spinning wheels with ineffective methods. With TAPS you don't worry about the competition, you become it.

A senior relationship manager for a large client in the Northeast, tells this story that illustrates what we mean:

> "I had met twice with the principal owners of a prospect business and was trying to schedule a third when the secretary/gatekeeper called to say they weren't ready to make any decisions for a number of practical reasons.
>
> "But she said that near the end of the year they wanted to start having serious conversations about what we had to offer them. She told me, 'We had several bankers come in and talk to us and all they said was, "We're the best. We're the local bank. They were beating their chests." '
>
> "She said, 'During your two and a half hour lunch with us, you didn't beat your chest. You focused on us.'
>
> "Just because of that, the principals wrote a letter to my manager telling him I had given them the best experience they ever had with a banker."

Chapter 7: Completing the Cycle

"Good fortune is what happens when opportunity meets with preparation."

—Thomas Edison

HARRY COLLINS WAS a legendary salesman for Frito-Lay who, over a long career, earned a wide reputation for persistence and success. He claimed he'd made 130 calls on one prospect in a single year before finally getting an order. Asked how many calls it would take before he'd give up, he said, "It depends on which one of us dies first."

To achieve success in banking, you don't have to outlive your prospects and you wouldn't call a prospect 130 times in one year. But the best and most efficient results do come to those who've planned well and execute consistently and relentlessly.

For one thing, the average sales cycle in banking—from initial prospect call to close—has expanded in recent years to an average of seven calls. Furthermore, at least 90 percent of prospects say they are satisfied with their current banking relationship.

Your job, and the goal of the TAPS system, is to prove to prospects that you are prepared to earn their business, that you're in it for the long haul, and you are prepared to offer more value than their current bank.

TAPS brands the bank as a true resource, not a commodity, and brands the banker as a "go to" person—a performance consultant. This takes time. It depends on the industry, but a good yardstick is advertising. It is well-documented that it takes an average of five or more "impressions" before most people even notice an ad, and if they are ever going to be tempted to buy, it takes several more exposures to the ad before a sale results.

Off-Peak Prospect Calls

If you still haven't gotten an initial appointment, and you haven't been able to speak to your prospect directly, we suggest leaving an off-peak voice mail on Thursday evening or Friday morning at the end of the second week of the cycle. This one final touch lets the prospect know you haven't forgotten them.

The later in the day the better. Voice mail is time stamped and anyone receiving a value-focused voice mail, maybe mentioning a new fact or trend in the client's industry, at 10:37 at night conveys a clear message that this banker really wants the business. Of all the components of TAPS, off-peak voice mails are used the least but they can be the most effective tool. Prospects are almost always impressed with the banker's long hours and tenacity.

Here's an example of an off-peak message:

"Mr. Johnson, I'm sure you would want your sales associates to reach out to one more key prospect every night before their heads hit the pillow. Tonight that's what I'm doing with you. I found a white paper about how trucking companies are managing their fuel costs and I'd like to bring it by. I'll be in my office tomorrow morning from 8:30 to 10 and again from 2 to 4 o'clock. Let's find a good time to meet. This is Becky Jones at National Bank, 888-123-4567."

Your Outbound Message

One aspect of prospecting that often goes overlooked is the impression you create when callers reach your voice mail system instead of you. When was the last time you listened to yours? Even if you have, it doesn't hurt to ask some associates or friends to call your number and give you feedback.

Your outgoing message (recorded standing in a quiet place) should have a sincere smile in your voice, make your identity clear, contain some sort of benefit statement, and be short.

Immediacy can be created if you record your message every day, mentioning the date and, if appropriate, any special message that might relate to a promotion or other information of immediate interest. But if you do this, it must be done ritually. Nothing turns prospects off faster than a message in July that begins, "Merry Christmas!"

Here's an example of an outgoing message:

"Entrepreneurs are always looking for ways to improve their performance. For a suggestion that can enhance your bottom line results, leave a message and I'll get it to you within 24 hours. This is Jamie Smith, the banker that gets things done at National Bank. Make it a great sales day."

Circle Back Strategies

Bankers who successfully subscribe to the TAPS process don't quit. After the initial two week cycle has been completed and there is no response (no yes or no) from the prospect, we recommend circle-back strategies to establish "mind traction" with top prospects.

How often you should reach out after the first cycle depends on the prospect. Some bankers divide the prospects they have identified into three sub-groups depending on potential. Group A should be contacted once a month; Group B, once every other month; and Group C once per quarter.

Every contact should offer the prospect some useful value, whether it's a news article, an industry study, an email link to an interesting web site, an invitation to a seminar, a Google news alert item, or some other information that is oriented to the customer and not the bank.

In addition to news alerts, Google also offers a free news feed function. You can establish a free Google homepage and set up sections to capture online news in any of a hundred or so industry categories. Each day, all day long, you'll get stories relevant to your prospects.

If your prospect is a woman, consider looking for interesting information on sites that cater to women in business. There are also resources devoted to any number of diversity markets—Asian, African-American, Spanish-speaking, and so on.

The D-Market—for Diversity—is the fastest-growing, hardest-striving segment of the population and smart banks understand that stale notions connecting diversity with poverty are false. Major banks doing business in Spanish-speaking markets like California, Texas, and Florida earmark a significant portion of their marketing budgets to diversity marketing.

Banks in areas where Asians concentrate have discovered that this is a booming and entrepreneurial corner of U.S. capitalism. Asians often have strong international family ties at a time when international trade is booming. Asians are changing the face of American business.

In the Philadelphia metro region, a highly-branched market, three Korean-language banks opened their doors in 2006–2007. The FDIC reported that deposits held by banks catering to the Asian market in Philadelphia alone doubled in the four years ended 2006, to $310 million. The FDIC forecasts the buying power of Asian-Americans to exceed $600 billion by 2011.

Any bank that actively prospects in a diversity market and does it thoughtfully and well is going to stand out.

Are We There Yet?

As a process, prospecting should be going on all the time in the context of a weekly and monthly rhythm. You identify five or so new potential prospects each week, and follow the steps outlined each week to move the prospects closer to the top of the funnel, and then down into it.

At the bottom are the conversations that resulted in sales.

Each banker should have a monthly calendar to keep track of the rhythm:

- **Five new letters go out each Monday.**
- **A note goes out to them on Wednesday.**
- **Emails or faxes go out on Fridays.**
- **First phone calls or visits take place the following Tuesday.**
- **Off-peak calls are placed on the second Thursday in the cycle.**

Bait Before Hooks

Earlier we described the process of identifying prospects as being similar to the way a big cat stalks its prey, looking for the best potential and patiently waiting for the right moment to spring. An apt metaphor for the actual practice of moving a prospect into the funnel is the way porpoises hunt sardines.

Sardines school in tight masses called shoals—a large dark cloud of fish swimming together. Sardines are far down the food chain and the species survives by reproducing in large numbers and traveling in enormous, dense packs.

In the world of banking, the sharks are your competitors who are blindly and without much thought pitching prospects.

Porpoises are air-breathing mammals who love sardines but can go only swim underwater a couple of minutes at a time without coming up for a breath. One way sardines avoid these predators is going deep into the water where the porpoises can't reach them.

Porpoises being smarter than sardines and most other sea creatures, they've figured out how to beat the fish at their own game. Rather than plunging into the cloud of sardines and grabbing a few before the whole shoal escapes into the deep water, the porpoises make noises they know will attract their own enemies—sharks. Sharks attack from below and soon they emerge from the deep looking for fresh porpoise.

But they are distracted by the shoal of sardines and attack it. While the sharks are plunging into the big cloud of fish, the porpoises work together to break up the shoal and isolate smaller groups of sardines that they then corral and polish off.

In the world of banking as we envision it, the sharks are your competitors who are blindly and without much thought pitching prospects with term sheets, products, special offers, and other shop-worn marketing tactics. You are one of the porpoises, letting the clumsy sharks—that came out to eat you—drive the sardines into your trap.

One of our clients is smart like a porpoise and illustrates this through the experience he had courting a prominent local business.

> "The other banks in my market are visiting the same prospects we are, but they are just throwing a term sheet on the table, saying, 'If you bank with us, we'll give you a loan for this much, for this many years.' One of the companies everyone is after here is a big food wholesaler."

> "Instead of talking to them about products, I had a series of meetings to discuss their business and learn how they operate. After five meetings, I still hadn't given them so much as a term sheet. But I learned a lot about them, including the fact that they were thinking about building a new facility in a new market. I introduced them to a

real estate broker I knew who would treat them well and help them find what they needed."

"I told the CFO, 'When you're ready to finance the new building, I'll give you terms.' He really appreciated it and we got the business while all those term sheets from everyone else went into the trash."

Successful banks of the future will be those that build and commit to supporting business consulting units with business development officers that don't operate on quotas but focus on relationships.

Any bank can offer transactional services, competing on rates and terms when a prospect or customer walks in with a need. But if a prospect comes to a banker about financing some machinery, the banker should be looking at it as a potential relationship to see what other transactions the prospect might need in the future. If they have no intention of moving their checking accounts and so on, it may not be worth trying to compete on price."

Back to Reality

The TAPS process of developing relationships with prospects may seem simple as we've sketched it out here, but in practice it requires discipline, creativity, and above all, good sales management. In our on-site programs and consulting, we work with bankers to help them learn the skills, establish the rhythms, and perfect the conversations. But we especially work with managers to teach them how to coach their prospectors.

The sales funnel is a hungry beast that demands constant feeding. While an individual banker can stand out in the crowd at a bank that doesn't institutionalize the prospecting process, he or she is likely to become frustrated in their career goals, and the bank is not going to achieve the results its shareholders and other stakeholders expect.

In Part III, we will discuss the challenges and opportunities for keeping the momentum up.

PART III
The Rolling Revolution

Chapter 8: The Sales Management Paradox

"[C]oaching and not direction is the first quality of leadership. Get the barriers out of the way to let people do the things they do well."

—Robert Noyce, founder, Intel Corp.

MIXED IN WITH his extensive experience in banking, Bob St. Meyer worked for several years as a salesman in the medical supply business. It opened his eyes to the opportunities banks overlook in sales management.

> "My sales manager in the medical supply business had no accounts of his own. He earned an override on what his sales people generated. As their sales went up so did his income, and vice versa."
>
> "I had, in effect, two managers working with me: one for the manufacturer of the disposable supplies and one who worked with the regional distributor. Both had a big stake in my success."
>
> "My company manager would sometimes

> travel with me," he recalls. "He'd coach me beforehand on what I needed to know and what I should be asking the prospect. We'd go in to a call and each of us played our roles. Afterward, we'd do a debriefing and he would make suggestions about how I could improve my conversations with customers. It was tremendously helpful.
>
> "In a bank, the people I worked for wouldn't have even been considered sales managers but were department managers who had portfolios of their own on top of managing other people. That is still typical today. As sales producers, they have to choose how best to use their time between meeting their own goals and quotas, and keeping track of others.
>
> "The multi-tasking bank sales manager tends to do the prospecting, establishing, and nurturing of the relationship and then hands it off to a junior person to execute the details. That's dysfunctional and no way to train sales people.
>
> "Managers have their hands full just managing relationships. They don't want to do the administrative work. Meanwhile, the expertise they have in generating new business doesn't get handed down to the junior people and the pattern is repeated."

We find very few banks have developed and institutionalized a system for coaching prospecting and sales skills the way credit skills are taught and reinforced. The expectations on the credit side are clear: if you do a bad job and cause the bank an avoidable loss, you're history. So a great deal of time and effort goes into coaching bankers how to manage credit, and little or none into coaching on prospecting. Thus, if you're a good credit-risk manager but you can't sell, the bank will find a place for you, even if you're a flop at the activity that pays the bills.

Planning to Manage

One of the greatest frustrations for St. Meyer & Hubbard, for other thoughtful industry consultants, and for the bankers who embrace the philosophy and techniques we teach is lack of vision or commitment by senior managers. Traditionally, people attracted to banking are those who like to serve. Banking now needs people who are active listeners, good at conversing with prospects and customers, and alert to sales opportunities. These two motivations—to please and to produce—are not always compatible.

> **Banking needs people who are active listeners, good at conversing with prospects and customers, and alert to sales opportunities. These two motivations–to please and to produce–are not always compatible.**

Some bankers even resent being recast as sales people. Industry observer Charles M. Wendel says most bankers, "don't understand who's paying them. It's changing, but slowly. The typical experienced relationship manager is in his or her forties or fifties. Their institutional knowledge is valuable but they acquired their habits long ago, before we began to ask them to be portfolio managers and outside sales people. They don't get the connection between what they do and how they're paid."

One of the solutions some banks have tried is hiring business development officers (BDOs) from outside the industry. They are the sharks that drive the shoal of sardines to the surface where the porpoises, the relationship managers, can catch them. These BDOs have no portfolios. All they do is beat the bushes—cold-calling and knocking on doors, getting names and contact information to pass on to what some banks call portfolio managers.

"I'm opposed to this approach," says Wendel, president of Financial Institutions Consulting. "Last week this man or woman may have been selling real estate or computers and this week it's banks. You want your best people in front of the client right off the bat, and the best people are the most experienced bankers."

Just throwing experienced people at prospects is not the answer, either. To manage a prospecting approach like TAPS and make it work well, banks must apply rigor and discipline to the effort, creating a consistent, trust-based system that rewards performance.

But in many institutions, RMs are free to create their own job descriptions. Says Wendel, "The typical commercial banker is often allowed to decide how much time he's going to spend selling and how much on administrative chores. You've got to have a system, so the RM is calling on screened prospects, primarily spending time on the portfolio and exploiting it as much as possible.

"But in a culture that is sales-driven (as opposed to relationship-driven), even exploiting portfolios can be a challenge. I've had bankers tell me, 'I've sold everything I can sell to my customers.' A good sales manager and coach would know to send this banker back to talk to customers about other aspects of their lives, such as wealth management and trust concerns, and for referrals."

Without structure, a system, and follow-through, bankers will follow the path of least resistance, spending their time trying to squeeze every last dollar out of their portfolio rather than devoting time to building new relationships.

Added Value vs. Value Added

Some banks have invested large sums in updating their customer relations management (CRM) systems—sophisticated software that gathers information and distributes it to those who can make the best use of it. CRM systems can, for example, alert a relationship manager when an existing customer deposits a large check, or it can produce lists of new customers so the bank can make a timely thank-you and survey call.

When Park National integrated the TAPS program with its ECM (enterprise customer management) system, they began to hear regularly from customers how startling and refreshing it is to have a bank reach out to find out if they were satisfied or had any others needs.

But the biggest investment in the best CRM systems in the world is no guarantee if the managers are not coaching and requiring the RMs to use these tools a part of a prospecting program. Prospecting is a way of life, a business belief system that emphasizes "value" over "added." Instead of promising value, great sales people deliver it without being asked. The "added" comes when that value translates into loyalty that leads to a purchase decision.

Prospecting is a way of life, a business belief system that emphasizes "value" over "added." Instead of promising value, great sales people deliver it without being asked.

We see no slowdown in the trend toward customers disaggregating their financial decisions. It's not unusual for a business owner to have a personal checking account with one bank, business account with another, investments with a brokerage firm, auto loan from somewhere else, equipment financing from GE, and so on.

Banks could get a lot of this business, but they have to come up with a good reason. One way to do that efficiently is to figure out which markets are likely to be your best and most profitable. A Barlow Research study found that being "easy" to buy from ranks high on the list of factors customers consider.

What Are You Good At?

There are three key competencies of a top-performing sales professional, according to Chally Group Chairman Howard Stevens. In his book, "*Achieve Sales Excellent*," a survey of 80,000 buyers and 200,000 sales people, found the leaders:

Personally manage customers' results, creating value through personal accountability.

Have a comprehensive understanding of their customers' businesses.

Advocate for delivery of the customers' expected results.

Banks can't be all things to all people, but they have one great advantage and that is they are local and visible. To compete well in the business market, bankers should consider positioning themselves as *performance consultants* in their core competencies.

If your bank has experience with professional services—law, accounting, medicine, and so on—why not specialize in that area and build a reputation for understanding their challenges? At a recent American Bankers Association marketing conference, it was estimated that this group is up to 10 percent more profitable than the average business client.

There are many ways to segment the market, including the diversity market we discussed earlier. When you pick your target market, it's important to remember that you also end up picking your competitors. Segmenting is a way to exploit markets that are under-served or where loyalty to the competition is weak.

It's also a way to leverage the knowledge you pick up as part of the TAPS process and getting to know your prospects and customers. If you know the real estate business backward and forward, and you're making your customers happy, the market will come to see you as the go-to institution, prospecting becomes easier, and sales cycles shorter.

Managing by Observation

Sales managers in the banking industry should do much more of what Bob St. Meyer's sales manager was doing for him in the medical supply business—getting directly involved with the RMs, listening to them and observing them—not only on joint calls, which is fairly common, but much earlier, such as when they are on the telephone attempting to obtain a face to face appointment. Are your RMs having a curiosity-generating conversation with the customer or are they falling into the bad habit of making a sales call—trying to sell a loan or some other product? Bad habits return quickly unless RMs are accountable to change their behaviors.

When you're asking bankers to go outside the norm, to break old habits, unless you observe them you won't know if they're doing what you want. This requires managers to lead and coach, and to do it consistently and supportively.

We know this works because we've made it work. One of our early clients was a major Chicago-based bank that decided to start a small-business banking unit. They had to start from scratch and used the TAPS system to get themselves going. But the managers, who had been terrific RMs before they were promoted, fell into the trap of many bank coaches, complaining that they didn't have the time to coach and that their RMs saw coaching as an intrusion.

Predictably, they were getting very low appointment rates—less than five percent. We came in one day and worked with four bankers, coaching them on their phone-calling techniques, doing the post-call debriefing, and so on. Lo and behold, by the end of the first day we had achieved a 20 percent appointment rate.

This is a common experience for us. We use an observation guide we developed, and monitored the bankers in three telephone appointment situations: a) collaborating with the gatekeeper, b) leaving an effective voice mail, and c) reaching the decision maker.

We listened to the bankers' behaviors during the conversations and coached them immediately after each call so they could adjust their approach on the next call to improve their "hit rate."

It is common for sales managers to make joint calls. It is unusual for managers to monitor RMs telephone calls. The observation guide used with coaching on telephone conversations invariably results in more face to face appointments.

Coaching Coaches

The first coaching we like to do with our clients is coaching the managers because they are the fulcrum of any culture. We can bring the RMs up to speed and get them on track with the best prospecting system, but as soon as we leave, they will tend to revert to old habits. That's because their managers are busy with credit and administrative activities, managing costs and meeting goals. And most of them have a portfolio of their own to manage.

Many sales managers got there by becoming a top producer. Promoting top producers to manager may seem to make sense but it is often a mistake. The typical top producer is inclined to continue to prospect and sell, and put coaching on the back burner. They know how to fish and don't want to have to stop to show others how it's done. Chally Group's studies find that only 15 percent of top sales producers make top sales managers.

Promoting top producers to manager may seem to make sense but it is often a mistake. The typical top producer is inclined to continue to prospect and sell, and put coaching on the back burner.

How do you teach someone to be a good observer and coach? For the approximately 85 percent of bank managers who have no experience in such leadership roles, it's a challenge. There is a natural suspicion of coaching as punishment for poor performers.

If you've come up through the ranks in an organization that has never made positive reinforcement an element of leadership, as a sales manager you are naturally going to see coaching as an unwanted burden. You're used to coaching when there's a problem.

The way around this is to make coaching a regular assignment for the managers and for the RMs to have the assignment of going to their managers to seek coaching. For example, RMs share their call plans with their managers each week. If the manager can't be there to observe the call, the RM is obligated to debrief the calls with the manager in person, saying what was accomplished.

Good vs. Right

We encourage sales managers to make this process mandatory, and we try to teach the coaches how to observe behavior. You've got to change the culture from the top down.

We find that most managers don't know what they're supposed to be looking and listening for when they observe. As a consequence they will go with an RM on a sales call and when they came back, their observation notes will say things like, "Good opening. Good questions. Need better listening skills. Poor presentation of solution. No close." These are all judgments and no specifics.

We try to explain to the managers that they have failed to talk about what was said, and they often look at us like we're speaking porpoise.

Instead of saying, "Good opening," managers ought to write about what the RM actually said. We want them to say to the RM, "Last time we talked about this prospect, you told me he was going on a vacation to Cancun. You could have asked him how his vacation was and make a personal connection."

So instead of "Good opening," we want to see coaches write down the first four words of every question to see if they were open or closed, and if they were logistic-level issues. You can't just tell a RM, "I want you to ask better questions." Your role is to be specific.

It's the same concept as in sports coaching. A football coach doesn't say to his quarterback, "I want you to throw more completed passes." He talks about observed, specific behavior with specific suggestions to get a better result.

To put it another way, it's as simple as the rules for raising a confident child. If a parent tells a child, "You flunked that test. You didn't study hard enough," you're sending a judgmental message—what's wrong with you? Instead, the message should be, "Let's look at that test you failed and see if we can figure out where you stumbled so that next time you won't make the same mistakes."

In banking, as in parenting, we're all busy and we tend to take shortcuts. We correct instead of teach. Instead, "Poor opening" can become, "How can you say that differently?" You want to focus on what was said, not on the character of the RM. That automatically puts people on the defensive.

You want to focus on what was said, not on the character of the RM. That automatically puts people on the defensive.

One way we get around this issue is that when we work with clients, we will often tell the managers the specific behavior we think is below standard, but we won't tell them who is having a problem. This often puts managers off at first. They are eager to know who isn't meeting expectations, who isn't getting it. But we feel having this information distracts managers from the big picture of putting together a team that can perform. It's not our role to evaluate individuals who aren't being obedient. Our job is to help banks create a culture of performance.

Managers who fail to observe behavior fall into the trap of generalization and judgment. We encourage them to prepare for coaching by setting up expectations and making the RMs feel safe. If the manager is going out with an RM on a joint meeting, they should have a short talk before hand and agree that, for coaching purposes, they are going to focus on a particular aspect of the conversation. We'll get more specific about this in our upcoming book on sales management and coaching.

Ask, Don't Tell

In our work we observe some common missteps that RMs make. Tone and word choice is common. They'll say to a prospect, "I just want to talk to you about..." and their voices trail off after the word "just." This is not an adult-to-adult conversation.

Lose the word "just." It's almost an apology when you have no need to apologize. Use active verbs and few hedge words. Speak in declarative statements. Then the tone changes, you're more in the present and you come off as more confident.

Another classic fumble is when the customer gives the first bit of resistance: "I'm happy with my present bank." The banker will often respond, "I not suggesting you should switch banks, but we can probably save you some money." It's a mistake to go into statement mode and although many bankers still do it, it's a very bad idea to open your prospect discussion with a discount.

Instead we recommend the RM go into questioning mode. "It sounds like that bank is important to you. What would you say makes a good relationship with a banker, and what are some mistakes bankers make?" If you want to persuade someone, first you have to ask and let them tell you their story before you can put a solution in their lives.

The more resistance you meet, the more inquisitive you should be. Engage the prospect in conversation. The greatest sales tool is the ability to listen for opportunity. We've talked a lot about that in this book, but it's so important it bears repetition: people want to be heard, seen, and understood. The ability to listen well is the most persuasive quality an RM can ever develop.

People want to be heard, seen, and understood. The ability to listen well is the most persuasive quality an RM can ever develop.

This is basic human nature, as Perle Mesta, the legendary Washington hostess and oil heiress, understood. She was once asked the secret of her success in getting so many wealthy and famous people to attend her parties. She replied, "It's all in the greetings and goodbyes." When each guest arrived she always said, "At last you're here!" And no matter when they left, she always said, "I'm sorry you have to leave so soon."

Chapter 9: Seeing Forest Instead of Trees

"Management is nothing more than motivating other people."

—Lee Iacocca

BUSINESS DEVELOPMENT is successful over the long haul when it becomes a way of life, an instinctive, action-oriented thought process. But the instinct does not come naturally or in a pill, nor is it created by adding more training events, the phenomenon known as "butts in seats."

Too many banks are "sheep dipping" their people through one training program after another, hoping one of them will provide the cure. The answer is not "training events", but the coaching that rarely follows. The soldiers may be well-armed, but their commanding officers need preparation to lead.

Increasingly across many different industries, there is a growing recognition that, like health, it is difficult for an institution to self-diagnose its problems and even harder to perform surgery on yourself. Furthermore, there is no such thing as a permanent "fix," and athletes rarely achieve excellence by training themselves. They need coaches, and they continue to need coaching throughout their careers. The same is true in banking.

All banks at one time or another hire trainers to come in and educate their RMs and other staff on the latest technology and concepts, or other aspects of the business. But when the training is over, even when the managers have signed on to a new way of thinking or doing, it's extraordinarily difficult to keep up the momentum. People have a tendency to backslide and the rate of recidivism is high.

No one understands this better than Bill Hippensteel, Senior VP, Director of Product and Segment Management at Compass Bank. "Training is important," he says, "but from company to company, we find there is little difference in the modeling technique to specific clients' needs. The key is getting your people to understand that every client is different and you need to understand those differences before you can be successful.

"Having outside coaches who listened to sales calls on the telephone and made joint calls on prospects in the field required the bank to remain involved in the ongoing process."

"What we learned through the TAPS process was that there was tremendous benefit in having an outside source with thoughtful insight to track results and provide continuing support. Having outside coaches who listened to sales conferences on the telephone and made joint calls on prospects and clients in the field required the bank at every level to remain actively involved in the ongoing process."

Hippensteel says follow-through was the key missing link for him. "It's one thing to sit people in a room and say, 'This is what you're supposed to do and expect people to walk out of the room and do it.' People forget new learnings unless they incorporate them into their life. It's like a golf lesson. A pro tells you what you are doing wrong and makes suggestions to adjust your swing. But the next time out, you're going to go right back to what you used to do unless there is someone observing and coaching you to do it the new way."

Not All Markets Are Equal

Bankers can work their tails off generating new business through any number of means and doing all they can to support their RMs who are on the front lines. But different people have different skills and interests and each market has its own idiosyncrasies.

Hippensteel recalls, "I'll never forget sitting with a bank president in a small community market discussing the opportunities for sales growth. When I asked whether there were opportunities in, for example, the gas station business, the bank president said, 'We've got everybody already.' And he wasn't joking. It was a small town and there were only so many gas stations. In a case like that, where growth opportunities are not so obvious, you have to adjust your strategy to fit the market. But it still takes a continuous commitment to be successful."

As Hippensteel learned and we have observed in our work, that continuing commitment can be a difficult sell. "When we began re-engineering our prospecting and sales processes, the sales managers asked me, 'Why do I need some outside consultant to tell my people what they already know they should be doing?'

"The problem was many didn't know what to do.

And those who did, were not as effective as they should be. Getting objective feedback and guidance about what works and what doesn't, proved invaluable.

"Once everyone embraced the program, they recognized the value in having someone involved who brought a wealth of experience from helping other banks. People were able to set aside their egos and territorial concerns, and see how through this different process, we could become a better bank."

Leading For Change

After many years and working with thousands of bankers, it's clear to us that people in sales must often be dragged kicking and screaming into the age of performance.

A senior Performance Executive for Business Banking at a large client bank, has studied this issue and reports,

> "We once did personality profiling of our sales people and learned that, on average, they are impatient, sociable, informal, and don't like process.
>
> "On the other hand, the sales effort needs consistency, reduced variability, and measurable performance-process—particularly in a large organization that's trying to leverage its assets. But it is difficult.
>
> "In our organization we instituted a lot of change—everything from the incentive program to the way we underwrite credit, taking away the authority in the field and moving it to a centralized location. This helped remove the problem of RMs giving more credit to one client over another just because they liked them.

> "To win people over was tough. We did it through a series of roll outs—first to the management team and then into the field, classroom style, where we had them practice for awhile, and then reinforced it in the field. Bank training budgets are small today and many institutions are doing more of this training on line through memos, email, conference calls, and webinars. These are all decent tools but I think something gets lost when you don't have the face-to-face investment."

"Unless you have the leadership and the follow through, the sales managers will lose momentum. It's basic human nature—when the cat's away..."

From time to time this senior banker talks to other banking leaders about this process and he advises them that unless the person who is head of business banking is on board and engaged, change will be a big challenge. He tells them, "You need to get the head of the firm on a pipeline call every Monday morning or you're wasting your time and money. Unless you have the leadership and the follow through, the sales managers will lose momentum. It's basic human nature—when the cat's away..."

Successful business banking leaders understand that they have to become more assertive in identifying those people who get it and those who should move on. This senior banker says,

> "We changed the incentive plan and made it more lucrative. We identified people who weren't going to make it by hiring a company to do personality profiling and we used Predictive Index.
>
> "We developed a bottom performer profile

and top performer profile. We didn't fire as many people as we could have, but switched them around and gave them other opportunities.

"We worked hard to win buy-ins by top performers who were key. It took a quarter to develop this new way of managing people, a quarter to roll it out, and a quarter or so to see results. It was a success in the end, but not easy in the process."

Coaching From The Top Down

Why is it so hard to change culture from tick marks to performance? The first excuse of sales managers is always, "I don't have the time." The second one is, "My good performers don't want me in their way."

In our experience those two excuses are related because most people have trouble understanding how to make change happen. They think they don't need to coach their top performers because they're not a problem. And they know that their bottom performers take up more management time. They wouldn't be thinking that way if banking sales managers were compensated the way sales managers are in many other industries, by sales overrides.

This is common sense. If your time is limited, and your compensation is tied to the success of your sales people, where will you get the most bang for your buck—by trying to drag the poor performers up from the bottom, or helping your self-starting top performers to do even better?

The proof of this becomes clear when we ask our clients, "Do you agree that you have the ability to coach your top performers to higher levels?" They almost always do.

Then we ask, "Do you believe that your people view

coaching time with you as a reward or punishment?" They typically have trouble answering that question, but there are only three ways you can feel about anything—positive, negative, or neutral. No one feels neutral about coaching. So the answer invariably becomes, "The top performers see it more positively than the bottom performers." So it's a reward at the top, and a punishment at the bottom.

Your top people should be your top priority, since they view coaching time with you as a reward and a chance for them to get ahead.

But when you look into how these sales managers spend their time, you discover that they've been loading goals on the top performers and spending their time with the bottom performers. They increase top performers' goals because they depend on those people to bring home the bacon. Then they spend their coaching time with the problem children who most times will not change their behaviors.

This exercise is always an eye opener for clients. We ask, "What's the worst that can happen to your team?" The answer, correctly, is "I lose my Most Valuable Player." If that would be a calamity—we agree it would be—then your top people should be your top priority, since they view coaching time with you as a reward and a chance for them to get ahead.

Start at the top and work down.

There are numerous benefits to letting laggards lag while you focus on your best performers. Your top people are less likely to leave because you are helping them make more money and feel important. But also, those who are farther down the ladder are either going to self-select themselves out of your bank, either by failing or quitting, or they are going to see your coaching as a means to improve their own performance. They will be pulled up from the top by the promise of the reward, instead of being pushed up from the bottom.

Meanwhile, by spending more time with your top performers, you as a sales manager learn what it is about top performers that makes them so good, and you can repurpose that knowledge in coaching your lower-level performers.

In this way, replacing a culture of obedience with a culture focused on performance leads people and organizations to success.

Keeping the Fires Stoked

In even the most progressive organizations, maintaining morale and enthusiasm day in and day out can get tedious. When fatigue sets in, and the troops aren't having fun, it's the sales manager's job to find a way to stoke the fires.

A smart football coach whose team is playing below par and sleep-walking through practice might surprise the team one day by staging a softball game. You have to mix things up a bit.

In banking, one way to break up the routine is to have your team get together one morning and have a prospecting contest. If the team reaches a certain goal (appointments, for example), you take them all out to a nice dinner or a ball game.

It's important to note here that this is not a contest of individuals, but a contest that requires a team effort. You want everyone on the team to learn and try new things and if they do, they'll get a reward.

A common mistake managers make is to think they are being good managers when they excuse one RM from a team chore because they are tired of it. This might be the instinct to be kind or to reward a hard worker, but if you've decided a chore is important for professional growth, you're doing the wrong thing by trying to be kind. Good leaders know that if their people are going to be successful, letting anyone wander off the team for any reason is going to hurt them in the long run.

By the Inch It's a Cinch, By the Yard It's Hard

The American psychologist and author Alfred J. Marrow once conducted an experiment in goal-setting at a clothing factory he operated in Virginia. He was trying to figure out how to fashion a system that would motivate new employees to reach certain performance standards.

Marrow took a group of new, unskilled employees and set a production quota that was hard to achieve, and gave the team three months to meet it. At the end, the group had missed the mark by about one-third.

He then took a second group, also unskilled, and set progressive goals, raising the bar a little each week. As the workers' proficiency increased, the goals were raised. At the end of the same period of time, the second team had met the ultimate goal.

This is basic human nature and we see how it works in everyday life. Babies learn to walk one step at a time. Home runs are great, but the game is really won by singles and doubles and good fielding and relentless pitching, inning by inning. TAPS success occurs one letter, one note, one conversation at a time.

It's the sales manager's job to observe when morale is sagging and figure out how to make prospecting fun.

It's the sales manager's job to

observe when morale is sagging and figure out how to make prospecting fun—change the perspective, shorten the cycle, lower the goal. Instead of setting a goal of getting 15 appointments for the month, make it three for today. Then celebrate that success. This creates a sense of urgency and the achievable result of immediate gratification.

When Pushback Comes to Shove

Our senior business banker in the Northeast tells the story of a young branch manager who was excited about one of his RMs landing a new loan prospect. "The prospect was a woman who owned a hair salon, and she was going to add a pedicurist, renovate the store—the branch manager assured me that her boyfriend was a contractor—and call it a day spa. She wanted to borrow $1.5 million.

> "I had to explain to this branch manager that this was not a business plan. A restaurant does not become gourmet just by adding truffles to their salads. I had to teach him that he's supposed to be the first line of defense against this kind of time-wasting prospecting.
>
> "The problem from a management point of view is that it's become difficult for banks to attract people with that depth of understanding. It's not seen as a profession. It falls into the category of, 'Maybe I'll go collect tolls on the turnpike or I'll be a branch manager for a bank.'"

His experience is not unusual. Junior sales people are eager to succeed and don't have the experience, without coaching, to detect real opportunity. Once they latch on to a situation, they are reluctant to let go, even when everyone in the bank is telling them, "We won't pass on that credit.

It's outside our parameters."

Instead, they'll go back and work with the prospect to see if they can find the loophole to get the loan done. Then they'll take it back up and again it'll get shot down.

A great sales manager makes sure he or she has coached the RMs well so they don't even bother trying to develop business that'll never pass the smell test.

Now they go to the boss and complain about the risk managers. "I can't get anything through these people. I have this great deal and they won't do it." The sales manager needs to recognize early on that even though it's the only deal in the pipeline, all the energy being spent on getting it done is stealing time from prospects with real potential. A great sales manager makes sure he or she has coached the RMs well so they don't even bother trying to develop business that'll never pass the smell test.

The Experience Gap

Our senior RM client with many years experience tells us that those who go into banking today at the branch manager level see it not as a career but a stepping stone.

> "People who I mentor all want to be sitting in my seat in the next sixty to ninety days. They want to go from being a branch manager to commercial lending business development overnight.
>
> "Or they see banking as part of their education to go into another business. One of my clients in the manufacturing business took a $20,000 pay cut to go work at a large bank for two years just to get experience under his belt.

> "You no longer have people who start out as tellers or, as I did, in the back office answering the phone. At another bank where I previously worked, I had to train new branch managers and business developers. We had a turnover of 20 branch managers every 6 months. I polled the class and only a third of the managers I was training had previous banking experience.
>
> "Among the two-thirds without experience were six women whose previous jobs had been store managers for Victoria's Secret. It's funny, but not. I called up the recruiting people who told me they figured that these recruits had experience with customer service so they'd probably be good candidates. I asked the recruiter to please stay out of Victoria's Secret."

He understood that this was no way to run a bank, and we agree. An outgoing personality counts, but too many banks do a poor job of screening and then they teach them the bank's way of doing things and pray for the best.

When to Fold 'Em

Sometimes you think you've hired eagles and trained them and coached them but discover that what you have is not really an eagle but a trained turkey. What criteria do you use to determine whether you groom them or broom them?

Almost every bank has a performance counseling process. It's a good thing to have but it's mostly needed because the RMs haven't been coached in a behavioral fashion. Even if you've coached people at a behavioral level, some get stuck on the idea that they are being paid to talk someone into buying something they don't need.

Some people are not natural hunters. They want to provide service. They get no joy from creating wealth through their own efforts. You reduce the number of people who fall into this category if you coach on a behavioral level.

This is another instance of managing wisely. There are only so many seats on the bus. If you hire bodies, that's what you'll get—bodies. You have to make sure you have the right people on the bus and then you have to make sure they're sitting in the right seats. There used to be many more seats on the banking bus, so the selection and coaching process becomes even more important.

You have to make sure you have the right people on the bus and then you have to make sure they're sitting in the right seats.

Chapter 10: Creating A Creative Culture

"You can never solve a problem on the level on which it was created."

—Albert Einstein

CREATIVITY IN THE banking industry may sound like an oxymoron, but in order to survive the onslaught of competition it needs to be a priority. Any commodity business faces this dilemma, the challenge of being one of four gas stations on a busy corner. Creativity is how McDonald's founder Ray Kroc turned plain hamburgers and French fries into billions, and how Starbucks' Howard Schultz turned coffee into an international phenomenon.

If the top-line executives of a bank are rigid and inflexible, everyone in the bank learns to adapt, or move on. This, more than any other factor, is what separates winners from losers in the battle for business. Creativity lives or dies at the top.

Bank executives who are hostile to change send a message down the ranks that results in the hiring of people who are hostile to change. When we talk to bankers about the value of coaching RMs on their prospecting conversations and tactics, some executives retort, "Well, at this bank we're all very experienced bankers and if someone needed to be coached, they don't belong at our bank."

What they fail to grasp is that even experienced bankers need defined processes for successful prospecting and sales. Otherwise, you end up with as many processes as people. It's impossible to develop a strategy that is uniform, integrated, measurable, and productive. It's the sales equivalent of a Chinese fire drill.

Some bankers know there is value in coaching, but they are afraid to call it what it is. "Just don't say it's sales," they'll tell us. They think of sales as persuading someone to buy something they don't need. Instead they want us to call it customer service, which is a misnomer, misleading, and betrays a lack of vision, commitment, and/or leadership.

Turning Failure Into Success

One of the creative opportunities that many bankers ignore is the chance to profit from failure. Instead of getting angry and griping that you worked so hard and how could your prospect do this to you, we encourage bankers to follow up with a pleasant phone call: "We appreciated being considered and would like to know why you chose the other bank and what you saw in our proposal that you liked and what you didn't." Then they send a follow-up letter that leaves the conversation open-ended. We call it the "11th Hour Letter," intended to keep the door open.

This is one of those often overlooked tactics that, from time to time, will result in actual business when a prospect experiences buyer's remorse or there is a change in circumstances. If you don't ask, you'll never know.

This has nothing to do with changing minds or trying

to muscle a sale. Your conversation should be conciliatory and open-minded. At the very least, you'll learn what the competition is up to and how you are perceived.

The psychology underlying this approach is basic. Your prospect will invariably be stunned by your graciousness and appreciate your efforts to improve yourself. They will sometimes think, "Gee, I feel bad about having to reject this person." They may even feel indebted.

You should be asking the same question when you succeed. Incredibly, very few bankers do this. "We appreciate your choosing us and would like to know why you did, and why you didn't choose the other guys."

Another valuable conversation to have with existing customers is to ask who among your competition has been calling on them and what they're pushing. Bankers don't like to do this, thinking it somehow draws attention to the other guys, or might put them on the defensive. What they fail to grasp is that, so long as the tone is truly one of curiosity and not paranoia, your customer is going to feel important and is going to understand that you value their business.

Another valuable conversation to have with existing customers is to ask who among your competition has been calling on them and what they're pushing.

Never, under any circumstances, should any conversation with a prospect or customer include your disparaging remarks about the competition—or anyone else, for that matter. Always respond to disparaging remarks by your prospect with neutrality or objectivity. Assume that everything you say will end up in the ears of someone you wouldn't want to hear it and you'll save yourself from embarrassment time and again.

Taking The Market Temperature

Market research is an essential tool for many industries and banking is no exception. If you are responsible for helping RMs with prospecting, you should be studying both your market and your industry. You may be surprised by what you learn.

For example, a 2007 study conducted jointly by *Business Week* magazine and Capital One unearthed some interesting opportunities:

Half of small businesses (ten or fewer employees) feel under-valued or unappreciated by their banks.

A quarter of small businesses say raising capital and financing are their most difficult growth issues.

Three-quarters of small businesses finance themselves through personal savings, credit cards, loans from friends, and investment by employees.

Only one percent regard their lender as a trusted adviser.

This was driven home to us by an incident at a Small Business Banking Conference in Chicago in 2007. One of the sessions included a panel of small business owners, one of whom Jack asked to speak about her relationship with her banker. She talked about how he spent a lot of time with her at lunches and dinners, and what a "nice" person he was.

But when she was asked who her trusted advisor was, her banker wasn't it.

"My American Express OPEN rep is really my most trusted advisor," she said. "When I talk with them, I feel like they care about me. When I talk to my banker I feel they care about loans and products. You don't build a business around products, you build it around customers."

Carrot vs. Stick

We encourage sales managers to experiment with creative ways to reward successful performance that help build teamwork. One large national bank we partner with set up levels of goals—bronze, silver, gold, and platinum. The idea was to create a sense of shared purpose as opposed to singling out who was best and who was worst—to create a sense of individual accomplishment within a group structure.

If you know you'll be rewarded for playing against yourself and improving your performance, that seems achievable and success makes you feel empowered and motivated to keep improving.

Bronze was achieved when an RM reached a basic level of results. Silver was awarded when an RM reached a target goal that was considered ideal. Gold was awarded to those RMs who exceeded their silver-level goal. Platinum was for those who met the highest possible standards. The system was set up to reward progress as opposed to absolute performance. The results were made public each month and allowed a lot of people to feel good about their contribution to the overall effort.

The bank was startled when more people than they budgeted for had exceeded their previous results and were entitled to an expense-paid weekend get-away. They had to redo the budget and a month later they had to redo it again because so many of their RMs were striving to succeed. In the end, instead of 15 percent beating their personal best, they had 40 percent.

This is another example of simple psychology. If you have to compete in a golf tournament against Tiger Woods, you're going to give up before you begin. How can anyone play golf as well as the top guy? Why bother? But if you know you'll be rewarded for playing against yourself and improving your performance, that seems achievable and success makes you feel empowered and motivated to keep improving.

Bank sales managers that do this well can track and measure activity levels, and evaluate whether a particular RM's prospecting activity is paying off and where it may need adjusting. For example, we ask managers to review the average deal size of their bankers and compare that to their close rates.

If the goal is $10 million in new business and the average deal size is $500,000, the banker needs 20 new relationships to hit their goal. If their close rate is 50% the banker needs to make 40 presentations. This can be reverse-engineered all the way back to the number of letters that need to go into the mail box if the banker expects to exceed their production goals.

That's how entrepreneurs think and it's important for bankers to begin looking at that type of math instead of how many calls were made. When a manager coaches at that level, the banker understands not only what they need to do to win, but how they need to do it.

Managers often fail to help RMs learn how to spend their prospecting time and how to track it. They look at sales alone. If an RM is making a lot of calls but not getting prospects into the pipeline, the manager needs to talk to him or her about planning better for calls and someone needs to go with them and watch them make the calls and identify opportunities for improvement.

Everyone wants to be on the winning team. Instead of beating up people for failing to reach their goals, the conversation should be about how each one can contribute to the group's success.

Managers often fail to help RMs learn how to spend their prospecting time and how to track it. They look at sales alone.

Tag Teaming

Tapping into internal prospecting opportunities is much more than just cross-selling. We've worked with banks who experimented with what they call tag teams that include business bankers, trust managers, and organization managers who talk about customers they share or prospects they want to target.

In some cases, tag teams mostly produce gossip that may or may not be helpful. We worked with one large bank that instituted a more formal approach, with a system to help its RMs. They prioritize who they are going to meet with and what they are going to talk about. They'll discuss a select group of prospects with a team of bankers and then come up with a strategy and tactics to move the ball forward. Conversations may include representatives from various bank departments, from credit card processing to wealth management.

In order for the team approach to work the organization needs to encourage trust. When teams don't function well it's because someone doesn't trust another partner on the team. To create trust, you have to give everyone the chance to get some benefit from learning.

It has to be more than talk, with action items that are

specific and measurable, followed up with a discussion about how a contact turned out. Where there are problems, the sales manager needs to get involved quickly and resolve them.

Trust-Based Selling

Prospecting and sales practices have evolved over the years, along with the lexicon of terms to describe them. At banking schools and conferences where we speak, we suggest that while there was once a place for the now-popular term "consultative" or "needs-based" selling, a better way of thinking about the process is trust-focused.

What's the difference? Author and consultant Charles H. Green is credited with helping popularize the notion of trust as the basis of successful sales relationships. We are big fans of his approach, memorialized in his book, "Trust-Based Selling," and discussed on his popular website, trustedadvisor.com.

With Charlie's permission, we include here his discussion of why we need to change the words and concepts we use in our business relationships.

> "Needs-based selling and consultative selling ask questions to define buyer needs so that the seller can alter or position the product to address those needs, thereby raising the value to the customer and the likelihood of closing the sale. This may sound stunningly obvious and commonsensical. To that extent, it's a tribute to the triumph over the old product-focused approach of convincing people they needed whatever it was you had to sell.
>
> "Product-based selling is far from dead [but]

the mainstream view among sales practitioners is that needs-based selling and consultative selling represent the state of the art, the high road, professionalism in selling.

"But it's just not true.

"Reading the consultative or needs-based books, websites or training programs, you'll find two beliefs—implicit or explicit—that limit the value of these approaches to selling. Those beliefs are:

"Their primary intent is to close the sale.

"A secondary intent is to qualify prospects.

"Those may sound obvious and benign as well, but look at it from the customer's side. Together, those two beliefs mean that if you're paying attention to me as a customer, it's only for as long as you think this transaction will result in a sale for you.

"That means:

"While you're definitely in it for you, you're only in it for me if it bodes well for you.

"While you're willing to talk about my needs, you're not willing to do so unless you see a sale close at hand.

"Either way, it certainly appears you don't have my interests very much at heart.

"There is another way. It's called Trust-Based Selling®. It says focus on buyer needs so that you can better articulate them and get them met. Period.

"You don't focus on their needs because it'll get you the sale. You do it so you can help them better articulate their needs and get them met. Period."

"You don't focus on their needs because it'll get you the sale. You do it so you can help them better articulate their needs and get them met. Period.

"You don't focus on buyer needs in order to screen out buyers who don't need what you have to sell. You do it so you can help them better articulate those needs and get them met. Period.

"The key difference lies in liberating sales from the transaction. Trust flourishes only when the quid and the quo have some blue sky between them. Screening at the transaction level screams, 'I only care about your wallet.' Trust-based sales screens at the strategic customer selection level, not the tactical transaction level.

"For needs-based or consultative selling to become trust-based, you need to migrate away from the tight leash of the transaction. Loosen up. Get free of the 'pay me now or I quit doing this consulting' mentality.

"Trust-based selling says, If you consistently do the right thing by your customer, then when your customer needs what you're selling, you'll get the first call. And you'll therefore make more money.

"The highest profit comes when you make profit a byproduct—not a goal—of a truly customer-centric sales process."

Amen.

Resources

WANT TO GET BETTER at prospecting and sales in general? Here are some resources that can be of great help.

Barlow Research, Inc., www.barlowresearch.com. Barlow Research is dedicated to providing market research and guidance to the financial services industry in areas such as micro business, small business and middle market banking. For further information contact John Barlow at 763-253-1832.

Benchmark Consulting, www.benchmarkinternational.com. Benchmark Consulting is a management consulting firm that improves the profitability of its financial services clients through the delivery of management decision making information and change management services to realize the benefits of business process changes. For more information contact, John O'Connor, Practice Manager, at 404- 442-4163.

Branch Manager Newsletter is a monthly publication targeting issues in operations, sales, customer experience and sales management for financial institutions. For further information contact, Lana Chandler, Editor at 303-343-0206.

Chally Group, www.chally.com, over 2,000 customers globally, providing solutions for improved candidate selection, employee and organization development, and to profitably increase sales performance. For further information contact, Howard P. Stevens, President at 1.800.254.5995.

Financial Institutions Consulting, Inc., www.ficinc.com focuses on issues of productivity and growth for a variety of financial services clients. The firm's emphasis of work is on achieving practical, bottom-line results based on quantitative and qualitative research and an in-depth understanding of industry dynamics. The company also offers an excellent, free newsletter. For more information contact Charles B. Wendel, President at 203-431-8330.

First Research, www.FirstResearch.com, provides industry intelligence in more than 225 industries. For more information contact Bobby Martin, President, at 919-861-0851.

MarketInsights, www.formarketinsights.com, is an information-based consulting firm specializing in the development of strategic solutions for the financial services industry. They provide an integrated suite of services designed to optimize existing networks and facilities, as well as to identify and prioritize opportunities for growth. For more information contact Joe Sullivan, President,, 773-348-7752.

Solonis, www.solonis.com, helps clients realize their strategic business objectives by delivering innovative technology solutions and services. Proprietary event-driven sales processes, a patented collection of customer strategies, and unique software that quickly and seamlessly enables dynamic, results-oriented sales strategies, For more information contact Ron Buck, CEO at 480-588-9870.

Trusted Advisor, www.trustedadvisor.com, offers speeches, seminars and a dynamic sales blog featuring key issues in building trust-focused sales conversations. For further information contact Charles H. Green, CEO at 973-898-1579.